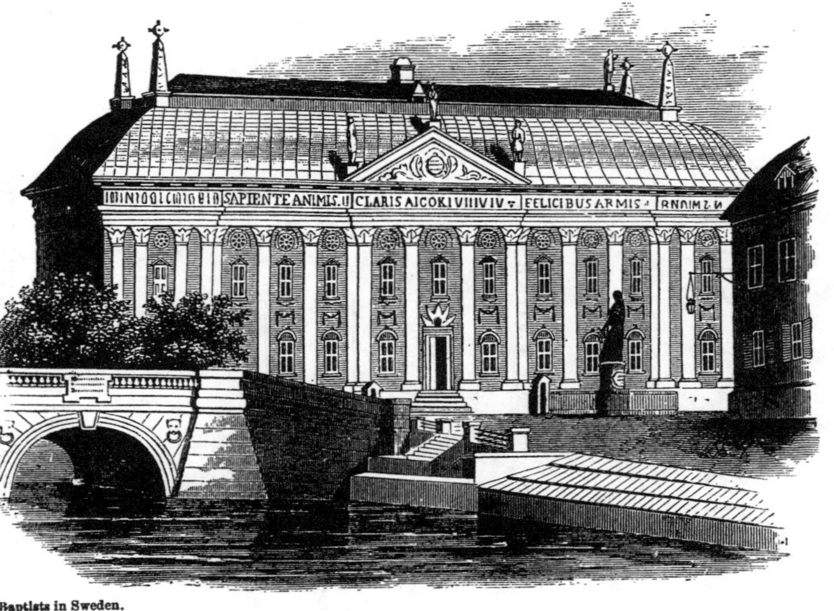

Baptists in Sweden.

HOUSE OF NOBLES, STOCKHOLM.

THE

BAPTISTS IN SWEDEN.

MRS. M. F. ANDERSON.

"The Lord hath done great things for us, whereof we are glad. * * * They that sow in tears shall reap in joy."—PSALM cxxvi.

Philadelphia:
AMERICAN BAPTIST PUBLICATION SOCIETY,
530 ARCH STREET.

This interesting book is affectionately dedicated, by the Publication Society, to J. WARREN MERRILL, ESQ., Boston, Mass., by whose liberality it has been stereotyped, and thus perpetuated.

CONTENTS.

CHAPTER I.

EARLY RELIGIOUS HISTORY OF SWEDEN.

CHAPTER II.

SWEDEN SINCE THE REFORMATION.

CHAPTER III.

THE SWEDISH DIET.

CHAPTER VIII.

DALECARLIA.

CHAPTER IX.

BAPTISTS IN DALECARLIA.

CHAPTER X

SKANIA.

CHAPTER XI.

ISLAND OF GOTTLAND.

CHAPTER XII.

WESTER NORRLAND AND ALAND.

CHAPTER XIII.

SWEDISH LAPLAND.

CHAPTER XIV.

PERSECUTIONS.

THE BAPTISTS IN SWEDEN.

CHAPTER I.

EARLY RELIGIOUS HISTORY OF SWEDEN.

SCANDINAVIA was among the last of the European nations that received the gospel of Christ. In the First and Second Centuries all of those nations that were under the control of Rome, were visited by missionaries of the gospel. Hence Italy, Gaul, Britain, and Spain received the word of God, before the rise of the Papal power, and were not, from the first, burdened with its errors and superstitions. Although the gospel was doubtless known to some of the inhabitants of Sweden at an earlier period, yet we have no account of the visit of Christian missionaries until the year 829. In that year Ansgarius, a monk from the monastery of Corbey, in France, braved the dangers of the journey, and entered Sweden, to plant there the doctrines and practices of the Church of Rome. It was at the earnest solicitation of King Biörn to Louis of

France, the son of Charlemagne, that this mission was undertaken. On the arrival of the missionary, he was welcomed by the king, who informed his council of the object which Ansgarius had in view. They gave him liberty to remain and prosecute his labors unmolested in the kingdom. It is said that several of the nobility were baptized, and that the prospects of the missionary were for a season quite encouraging.

But, among the people, there was still strong opposition to be overcome. The Swedes clung earnestly to their own religion, and were opposed to any change. Moreover, many of the Saxons who had been driven out from Germany when Charlemagne, by fire and sword, endeavored to convert them to Christianity, had fled to the nations of the north. They naturally bore with them a deep hatred to their conqueror, and to the religion which he had forced upon them. Their influence, of course, was exerted to hinder the work of Ansgarius. Accordingly, four years later, when Biörn was dethroned by his people, and driven out of his kingdom, and a new monarch seated in his place, a terrible persecution was experienced by the propagators and disciples of the new faith. It is said, by some writers, that the haughty and overbearing deportment of the missionaries who had come in, after Ansgarius left, was a prominent cause of this outbreak of popular fury.

In the year 860, when Ansgarius returned to

Sweden, it was necessary to commence almost anew the work. He found the king at Birca, and was once more allowed to preach throughout the land. It is said that his success in Birca was so great, that hundreds were baptized in a day. The king gave all of his influence to the spread of the new doctrine. But the resistance of Paganism was earnest and long continued; and beyond the immediate presence of the king and his court, the missionary met with little success. It was Romanism, rather than the gospel, which was preached; and the efforts of the missionaries were directed rather to make adherents to the Pope than converts to the faith in Christ. They were the representatives of a political power, which was gradually extending its sway, and preparing for the assumption of all the authority claimed, two centuries later, by Gregory VII. On the part of some there was indifference, on the part of others, opposition to their religious teachings; while the great mass of the people regarded with deep aversion their political mission. Thus another century rolled on.

At length Eric Arsaell came to the throne in 993. He embraced with zeal the doctrines of the missionaries, and favored their work. He himself is said to have been baptized at Sigtuna, and his example was followed by many of the chief men of the country. He commanded the heathen temples to be destroyed, the idols to be broken, and made it a penal offense to offer heathen sacrifices. But the hearts of the people had not yet been reached, and they were ill prepared for such an open and violent assault upon their ancient faith and worship. They rose in a popular tumult, and murdered the proselyting king in the year 1001, a fate which was shared by King Inge half a century later. Olave Skötkonung, who next secured the throne, was not deterred by the sad fate of his predecessor, from following the same harsh policy. He sent messengers to England to King Ethelbert, entreating him to furnish him missionaries for the prosecution of his work. The Papacy had already gained the mastery in the British Isles, and the missionaries who entered Sweden in answer to his appeal were, like all those that had preceded them, bigoted priests of Rome. On their arrival they proceeded to Upsala, where they gave instructions to the king, who listened with eager attention to their words, and was shortly after baptized by Sigfrid, in a spring that bears his name to the present day.

But, though much effort was made in the following centuries by the emissaries of the Papacy, the Era of the Reformation found the real religious condition of the people but little improved. A corrupt form of Christianity had come to supplant Paganism, and had nominally succeeded. But the real planting of the gospel was yet to be accomplished. The priests had striven mainly to gather wealth and power, and to bind the kingdom to the support of the Church of Rome. The history of the dignitaries of the Church was a history of wars and intrigues, as different from the history of the Apostles of the Lord as darkness is from light. The language in which a historian speaks of the reign of King Olave, may justly be applied to the whole of the period between his baptism, 1001, and the days of Gustavus Wasa, 1520: "The light of Christianity, or rather *the power of the clergy*, was spreading itself in Sweden." This sentence presents a brief epitome of the religious history of Sweden for five hundred years.

One remarkable instance, however, of the power of religious principle occurred to relieve the darkness of the picture of this period. During the tenth and eleventh centuries, the Scandinavian Vikings sailed far and near, gathering plunder and captives. Great numbers of slaves were brought from Germany, France, and England, into Sweden; so that the country was filled with them. In 1299 King Birger, son of Magnus Ladaslas I., came to the throne. The multitude of slaves brought the slave question before him at an early period in his reign. And this wise and pacific prince passed a law which shed lustre on his name and reign. He prohibited the sale of slaves in Sweden, on the ground "that it was unjust that Christians should sell each other, when Christ had made us free at the price of his own blood." This law indicates, on the part of the king, some proper understanding of the principles that underlie the gospel, and some conscientious desire to carry out the spirit of its teachings.

But the ignorance of the mass of the people was necessarily great. It could not be otherwise with their scanty means of enlightenment. Preaching never was a prominent part of the work of the priests of Rome, and their religious worship was offered in an unknown tongue. It was not till the year 1441 that a decree was issued requiring that the Lord's Prayer, the Ave Maria, and the Apostles' Creed should be translated into the mother tongue, and repeated on Sundays and holidays by the priests in the churches, for the instruction of the people. A few years later the Bishop of Linköping commanded the clergy of his diocese to introduce their services by the Lord's Prayer, the Apostles' Creed, the Ave Maria, the Ten Commandments, and the Seven Works of Mercy. With such scanty means of instruction, the religious knowledge possessed by the people must have been exceedingly limited. And as in other places, so in Sweden, it was found that "for the soul to be without knowledge it is not good."

A recent historian gives a sad picture of the morals of the time: "Concerning the general morality of the people, we hear the echo, in 1412—when the Council of Arboga was held—of complaints of the lewdness, rapine, murder, usury, contempt of penance and the Lord's Supper, and a mock of religion which satisfied itself with outward forms that sufficiently indicate the spirit of the age. The judgment so passed is not to be considered as the ordinary condemnation of the mere casual exceptions to good order. In like manner, the care which the Swedish church, in the middle ages, gave to the interests of the Lord, was not calculated to accomplish the transformation of a heathenish into a Christian people. Its righteousness of the law could not restrain and check the natural pride of the heart, or only so long as compulsion rendered necessary a specious submission. This compulsion kept pace with the Papal hierarchy, and necessitated more than once, both nobles and people, with weapons in their hands, to protect their human and Christian rights against bishops and priests."*

The author from whom the above is taken, himself a native of Sweden, in high authority, adds one sentence of strong condemnation upon all that had yet been done, at the end of the fifteenth century; "Heathenism, therefore, in fact remained, only modified by a Christian form of public worship, or a form of Christian superstition."

After all the efforts made from the days of Ansgarius, till the beginning of the sixteenth century—a period of seven hundred years—such were the total results. At this latter epoch the Church had become a powerful political engine; and the people were awaking to a consciousness that it was a

* Anjou, Ref. in Sweden, p. 50.

grievous burden on the kingdom. The worldliness and rapacity of the clergy were producing effects in Sweden, similar to those witnessed in other countries.

It will be interesting to notice more in detail a train of circumstances which finally led to the overthrow of the Papacy in Sweden. It will thus appear how, in the providence of God, evils work their own cure. A prominent cause of the destruction of the Papal power, was the conduct of the Archbishop, Gustavus Trollé, whose atrocities exasperated the minds of the people, and whose name, till this day, is held in execration in his native land.

In 1513, on the death of Suant Sturé, the administrator of Sweden, an election was held by the Diet, at which two prominent candidates for the office were put forward. One of these was Eric Trollé, the father of the young Gustavus,—then a student at Rome,—the other was Sten Sturé, the son of the former administrator. The clergy were unanimously in favor of the former, but the senators, the nobles, and the deputies from the provinces were favorable to the latter. On the 21st of July he was declared to have been duly elected. It was in the midst of political troubles that he entered on the duties of his office. Christian II. of Denmark, was pressing his claims to the throne of Sweden, and drew to his aid the clergy, who ordinarily took the part of the Danes in their struggles for the supremacy in Sweden.

Soon after his election, Sturé had consented to the withdrawal of the aged Archbishop, and to the election of Gustavus Trollé in his place. This was regarded as a compromise, a sort of compensation to the house of Trollé for the defeat of Eric. No sooner, however, had Gustavus, after his consecration at Rome, returned to his native country, than he settled himself at Upsala without calling on the Administrator at Stockholm. Here he commenced systematic efforts for the overthrow of Sturé, and the establishment of the power of Christian the Dane. He was, from the first, preparing the elements of a civil war. He fortified himself in his castle of Stecka, and prepared to wield all of his power for the benefit of Christian. He endeavored to induce the King of Denmark to enter Sweden, and promised that the Governors of the fortresses of Stockholm and Nyköping would open their gates to him. Sturé in the mean time adroitly drew from Arcimbold, the Papal Legate, all that he knew of the secret policy of the Archbishop, and proceeded at once to action. He arrested the Governors of Stockholm and Nyköping, and besieged Trollé in his castle, which he finally captured. In conjunction with the Diet, he took active measures which finally resulted in the deposition of Trollé from the Archbishopric, and in the demolition of his fortress of Stecka, and, it is said, in his own confinement in the castle of Westeras. Indeed, the people were so highly exasperated by his treachery and insolence, that they were with difficulty restrained from putting the hated prelate to death.

In the mean time Christian, at different times, invaded Sweden with a large force; but was constantly repulsed. At length, in 1519, another army under the command of Otho Krumpen, one of his generals, entered Sweden. Sturé went out to meet him; and joined in battle with the invaders. In the heat of the conflict he was mortally wounded by a cannon ball, and was carried to Strengness, where he shortly after expired. The people were thus left at this critical juncture without a leader. The nobles proposed to elect a new administrator; but the clergy took every means to prevent an election. They wished to prolong the period of weakness and uncertainty. In the mean time the deposed Archbishop came forth from his hiding-place, and boldly assumed once more his office. He plotted and planned until he succeeded in securing a Diet to meet his wishes. This packed Diet met and proceeded to choose Christian of Denmark as King. Christian, however, was not satisfied with an election in this form. He therefore convened the Prelates and Senators at Stockholm, and demanded his recognition as their lawful hereditary monarch—a demand which was subsequently made to the deputies of the people also. By both bodies the demand was conceded.*

Great preparations were made for his coronation, which took place a few days later, in the cathedral at Stockholm. On this occasion Gustavus Trollé officiated. No sooner was the government thus placed in the hands of Christian, than a cruel plot was formed by him and his advisers against the prominent men of Sweden. In order to guard against any further difficulty with the nobles of the land who had been unfriendly to Christian, Diedrich Slagheck, one of his ministers, recommended their indiscriminate slaughter. Desiring to accomplish his end with some pretext of law, Christian called to his aid his willing tool, Gustavus Trollé. The Archbishop readily consented to bear his part in the disgraceful transaction. He appeared as public accuser. In presence of the people he charged the nobles with having illegally deposed him from the Archbishopric, and with sundry affronts offered to certain of his clergy; and then demanded of the King their speedy punishment. As encouragement to the King, he assured him that by this act "he would draw down a recompense from God and the universal praise of Christendom." The King appointed a tribunal of ecclesiastics devoted to his wishes, who, of course, pronounced the judgment before decreed by him. The

* Mallet, Histoire de Dannemarck, tom. vi. p. 468.

Bishop of Strengness, the Bishop of Scara, Senators, noblemen and citizens, were led out as felons and traitors to the scaffold. Their bodies, to the number of ninety-four, were heaped around the scaffold, and the place of execution was overflowed with their blood. This gross outrage has left an indelible mark upon the hearts of the Swedish people. It was one of the prominent means by which the doom of the Papacy was sealed in that kingdom.

In the following year—1521—Gustavus Wasa, whose father, Eric Wasa, was among the number of the slain, raised the standard of revolution in Dalecarlia. It was a struggle both against the Danish King and the Romish prelate. Certain it is, that political considerations alone would amply have justified him, in the day of his triumph, in rooting out the power of the Papal hierarchy. His triumph, after a brief but severe contest, was the end of the Danish dominion and of the Papal supremacy in Sweden. The power of the priesthood was steadily, systematically weakened. Gustavus Wasa was resolved that the power of the priest should no longer come into conflict with the interests of the King. Several letters passed between him and Pope Adrian VI., who had succeeded to Leo X. The King assures the Pope that he was ready to respect all the privileges of the church, "if only the Apostolic See would appoint such bishops as were content with their limits and had a care for peace and harmony among the King's subjects—such as so vindicated the privileges of the church that they did no harm to the crown."

The Pope had demanded the restoration of the odious Trollé to his ecclesiastical dignities, and was unwilling to make any terms unless that point was gained. Gustavus replied indignantly to the demand. "He was surprised that the Apostolic See takes this bishop, the foremost coöperator in the godless murder of nobles and bishops, under its protection, and wishes again to place him on the pinnacle of the Swedish Church, whose liberties he has thrown to the ground." "It were a grief to us," he adds, "that the Apostolic See could not avenge the murder of the bishops. But still less can we endure that this archbishop should return to Sweden, who is not only unworthy of the priesthood but of life itself." His language next rises to the dignity of solemn protest, and when Gustavus Wasa used such words they were full of meaning. "We acknowledge ourselves to hold in such high reverence the holy Roman Church, that we would willingly offer our blood and life for it; but this act of severity which threatens our commonwealth with such disasters we shall endeavor to arrest, with our blood if so required, and will show, if it be necessary, in the face of all Christian princes, how justifiably we have resisted such an outrage." He concludes by courteously intimating that, if the Pope does not recede from his demand, he will dismiss his Legate from the kingdom "in order to announce, in that manner, as a consequence of the tardiness of the Apostolic See, the Swedish Church shall be reformed by our royal authority; * * * *since it is altogether necessary, and the sooner the better, that a reformation should take place in her spiritual and temporal condition.*"*

It would not seem that a prince so bold and plain spoken could long remain in subjection to the Papal yoke. The work of separation went steadily forward. The New Testament was translated; the discussion of its truths continued, at least among the clergy; the Scriptures were coming to be regarded as the final appeal in all religious inquiry; the foundations of the Roman Catholic system were thus gradually undermined.

At the Diet of Westeras, in the year 1527, Protestantism was virtually established; the bishops were stripped of their pomp, the churches of their immense estates, and an open way was left for the preaching of the gospel. The King, in his opening address, stated that he "together with many learned men, both within and without the land, had become convinced that the crown, nobles and people, were in many ways cheated and oppressed by the men of the church, who raised themselves to be masters, humiliated the princes, nobles, and people of the

* Anjou, p. 95.

country, and by their own self-devised forms of worship, by mortgages, sales, and other contrivances, heaped up riches so that the Crown and nobles had scarce a third part of what the priests, monks, churches, and cloisters had." It is estimated that nearly twenty thousand farms and homesteads were taken from the Church, and restored to the heirs of the donors, transferred to the Crown, or appropriated to charitable purposes.

The work in Sweden was a reformation rather than a revolution, and advanced by gradual steps. The Papal party struggled long for their privileges. The Jesuits labored hard to restore the ancient order, and at one time with a fair prospect of success. But at length, on the 25th of February, 1593, the Council of Upsala met at the call of Charles, Duke of Sudermania, acting Regent during the absence of King Sigismund. The Council declared that the confession of the Swedish Church consisted of the Holy Scriptures, the Apostles', the Nicene and the Athanasian Creeds, and the Augsburg Confession. All of the Council arose and declared that they would abide by this Confession, and be ready for it to stake their lives and blood. On this, the President of the Council, Nicolaus Olai Bothniensis, exclaimed with a loud voice: "*Now is Sweden become one man, and we have all one Lord and one God.*"

Thus was completed, for the Swedish people, one of the chapters of their religious history.

CHAPTER II.

SWEDEN SINCE THE REFORMATION.

THE Reformation in Sweden was an external work, proceeding rather from the policy of kings and nobles, than from the religious convictions of the people. It resembled rather the Reformation in England than that in Germany. And hence in both countries the changes in the organization of the Church were as slight as possible. In both, the prelatical power was retained. The work was wrought without any deep religious feeling among the mass of the people; and that same comparative indifference would seem to have continued for more than two centuries.

In devotion to the external form of religion, the country has not been wanting. Sweden has rendered good service to the cause of Protestantism in Europe in its hour of need. She can point with pride to the bold daring of Gustavus Adolphus, the champion of Protestantism, when the armies of the Papacy were seeking to crush out the Reformation. His bold achievements, and his death on the field of Lutzen, must ever occupy a prominent place in the external history of Protestantism. Yet notwithstanding all of the service rendered to the cause of the Reformation, the people were comparatively indifferent to the spiritual claims of the gospel. The usual consequences of the union of Church and State were experienced in Sweden, as we shall see after a brief glance at the organization of the Church.

The Lutheran Church, which was established by law in Sweden, differs in its organization from that in Germany. It is governed by diocesan bishops, of whom there are twelve, including the Bishop of Upsala, who is Archbishop of Sweden. He does not exercise, however, any metropolitan power over the other bishops ; he is merely first among equals. He presides over the House of Clergy in the Diet, and consecrates the other bishops, except when that right, for special reasons, is transferred to one of the others.

To each separate congregation there belongs a Consistory or parish council, composed of the pastor of the church, who acts as president, his assistant ministers, if he have such, and not less than four, and not more than eight, respectable inhabitants. This Consistory has power over a number of cases in the congregation, such as immorality, non-attendance on public worship, or the communion, matrimonial discord, and like offenses. It is also this council in whose hands has recently been placed the power to prevent conventicles.

There is also a diocesan Consistory composed of

the bishop and his provost, and other prominent men, a majority of whom must be of the clergy. They have the right to try matrimonial causes, and the offenses of the clergy, subject to an appeal to the civil power.

The king and the royal house, the officers of government, and members of the Diet, must all belong to the Established Church. The State and the Church are inseparably connected. The possession of many civil rights belongs only to members of the Church. The rite of marriage can only be celebrated by the clergy of the State Church, and only to those who are in her communion. The right to give evidence in a court of justice is forfeited, unless the witness has taken the communion within the year preceding. A certificate of communion is demanded of laborers and of servant-maids, in order to secure a place.

"The Lutheran Church of Sweden," says Dr. Edward Steane,* "is, perhaps, the most despotic ecclesiastical body in existence, not excepting even the Papacy. It binds its members to absolute and unreasoning submission, and is intolerant of the action of conscience without its pale and within. And its power is as ubiquitous as it is dominant. It follows a man into all the circumstances and relations of life, and leaves him a free agent nowhere. The youth cannot be apprenticed, the

* Evangelical Christendom, Oct. 1858.

young man cannot set up in trade, the citizen cannot become a member of any secular society as a trade, corporation, or city guild, a maid-servant even cannot change her domestic service without the permission of the clergy. Under heavy civil penalties, every infant must be baptized at the Lutheran font. Every child at the prescribed age must be confirmed, and every confirmed person must at least once in the year take the sacrament. A parishioner may not change his residence into another parish without the clergyman's permit; two parishioners of different parishes may not intermarry, if either of the two clergymen refuses a certificate; in short, there is literally almost nothing in secular life or domestic, as well as religious, which a Swede is free to perform without an interference of some sort from his Church. A crime is committed if any other person than a clergyman ventures to expound the Scriptures, or if a number of persons meet among themselves for reading and prayer; and if this should be done on the Sunday, the law convicts them of a double offense. Not that such meetings do not take place, or that laymen, in some instances, at least, do not make known the way of life; but these things are done at the peril of the parties, who, in many cases, have been severely punished."

A Lutheran pastor in the province of Småland unfolded to Mr. Brace the Swedish theory of Church and State, and the subsequent conversation brought out distinctly one of the evils of the system:

"'The State commences as a Christian State. It demands that all its members shall be Christians. For this purpose, it exacts that all who wish to be citizens shall pass through the outward rites of our holy religion. Every one must be baptized. Then, for the same reason, it requires that every one shall be instructed and approved by the pastor, and *confirmed* in Christian doctrine. If he cannot show the evidence of this instruction, his *Schein*, (confirmation papers), he is presumed not to be worthy of the privileges of citizenship. You see our stand-point?'

"'But do you not see,' said I, 'that you gain no real Christianity by this? You get outward ceremonies and conforming—that is all. And more, you are far more liable to cultivate hypocrisy than true faith. I should expect a Church, under such a system, to be lifeless.'

"'Ach! Sie haben recht! You are right. Our beloved Zion is almost *todt* (dead) now. But that is the result of other causes. In this system which you deplore, we at least gain that every man and woman and child shall be instructed in the principles of our holy religion.'

"'I would not discuss here the subject of public instruction in religion,' I answered; 'but in our view, the partaking of the Lord's Supper is a testimony of certain states of the heart with which law can have nothing to do. To enforce it under civil penalties, is to *command* the faith of the heart, which cannot in its own nature be subject to law.'

"'Es ist ganz recht! It is quite right!" burst in one of our party, Herr T., a very generous, impulsive young man. 'The Herr Americaner has hit it. I confess to the Herr Doctor (the Pastor), I suffer from this every year. The Herr Doctor will remember that I was confirmed before I could really understand these doctrinal problems. Now, it is the law that I must attend public Communion once at least a year. But I cannot. I do not care for it. I do not believe all the words which are said to me there; and yet I must. If I should stay away, that infamous N—— would inform against me, and I might lose my business, and be fined heavily. Is that right, Herr Doctor? I am a hypocrite!'

"The doctor was perplexed, . . . but for the time he took refuge in the easy assertion that the Herr T. should try to make the blessed Abendsmal (Communion Supper) reality and nourishment to himself, and then the yoke would be easy and the burden light."*

Let us now consider more fully the condition of the Church as delineated by different authorities. One who had special opportunity for learning its real condition, says: "It is difficult to exhibit the

* The Norse Folk, p. 378.

disparity in Sweden between the religious appearance and the reality, without giving offense to those who consider religion to consist in orthodoxy, profession, and church order. In general it may be said that religion is considered rather an ecclesiastical than a personal matter, and is confined within the doors of the sanctuary, to be solemnly assumed on entering there, and left behind when the threshold is crossed at the close of the services."*

Dr. Krümmacher, of Berlin, who has long been familiar with its history and condition, is said to have described the Swedish Church as an "ice-palace"—beautiful, glittering, but cold. A traveler in Sweden, accustomed to the religious associations of Scotland, says: "The clergy and the people appear to me to view Christianity altogether in a different light from that in which we view it. It is a different species of religion here. This is a subject on which I give my impressions with reluctance from the difficulty of explaining them. The Swedish clergy are, beyond doubt, a highly-educated body of theologians. The people also are educated, up to a certain point; which is, that of being able to read, and give proof of understanding the Church Catechism so well as to be entitled to Confirmation, and to be received as communicants. Here the working of the establish-

* Rev. Geo. Scott.

ment on the people seems to stop. A careful attendance upon all the ceremonies of the Church; the saints' days, or prayer days, or church festival days; the high mass; the forms of baptisms, christenings, sacraments, funerals; the decorations of the church and altar, and of the priests' robes; the Easter offerings, Christmas offerings, and such observances, appear to stand in the place of all mental exertion or application, on their part, in religious matters, after they have once, if I may use the expression without offense, taken out their diploma as Christians by the rite of Confirmation, and by receiving their first Communion. Religion seems to rest here."*

An extract from another more recent traveler will give some idea of the manner in which the Catechism is learned.

"He visited the school, [in a manufacturing district in the West of Sweden]. There were fifty-three scholars in it, with a rather stupid-looking old man as teacher. All the children were bawling out their Catechism together, evidently with no more idea what the sacred words meant than if they had been Indian incantations. And this is what the Swedes everywhere call 'teaching religion.'"

"As we went out, the Englishman [employed in the mills] said: 'You see it haint here just as it

* Laing's Tour in Sweden, p. 248.

is in our countries. They don't know much about all that; but they have to be Confirmed, helse they couldn't be citizens or any thing else, and they goes into the Sacrament as a sort of business, you know. Perhaps some of 'em really feels it, poor creatures! but I don't think the most of them cares or knows much about it. They leaves it to the parsons.' "*

" He visited another school in company with the gentleman who had established it for the children of the peasants.

" 'The truth is, Herr B.,' he said, 'I was driven into that school by the stupidity of the clergy. We had too much catechism in their school.'

"I told him my own observations confirmed what he had said. Everywhere I found a mechanical drilling in the words of theology, and certain dry facts of Biblical or Jewish history; and this was dignified by the name of teaching religion, though it evidently had no more connection with religion than with topography.

" 'Do you not meet with much opposition from the clergy?' we asked.

" He replied that he did. Some cried 'Infidel!' Still he was determined to carry the thing through. If the people were ever to be enlightened, the schools must be a little more in harmony with the times. The priests seemed to think nothing was

* Brace's Norse Folk, p. 219.

for a moment to be compared with their catechisations."*

The general impression which is left on the mind of travelers in regard to the working of the church system, may be seen from the following extracts.

"In no country," says Laing, "are the exterior forms and decencies of public worship better attended to. The churches are substantial, and not merely well kept up, but even decorated inside and outside; and there is a kind of competition between parishes for erecting elegant structures for public worship. The clergy are fairly endowed, well lodged, and in general on good terms with their flocks; they are also well-educated men, and form a body of great power in the state, the Chamber of Clergy being one of the constituent parts of the Diet. Yet, with all these exterior signs of a religious state of the public mind, and with all the means of a powerful Church Establishment, unopposed by sect or schism, to make it religious, it is evident from the official returns of crime, that in no Christian community has religion less influence on the state of morals. The just inference is, that no spirit truly religious has ever been generally kindled in this country."†

Mr. Brace, alluding to the same subject, introduces the opinion of some of the nobility of Swe-

* Norse Folk, p. 232. † Laing, p. 125.

den, who may be supposed to have a fair opportunity of forming a correct judgment.

"In our conversation we spoke of the clergy, and I found the same serious dissatisfaction with them here as everywhere. The Count thought that the support of the clergyman should come from the State, and then he would not be falling into those eternal bickerings with his people for every dollar of his stipend. It appears he is entitled to certain *pro rata* portions of the produce of his parishioners, and also expects gifts to a large amount; so that from this man he claims his one-tenth of corn, from that his one-sixteenth of barley, from another his two chickens, or leg of mutton, or eggs, or flax. Where there is love to the pastor, these all come in gladly and easily; but where there is not, he must be continually on the look-out, lest he lose something. When a poor creature comes, inquiring what he shall do to be saved, his first thought may be, 'You owe me seven bushels of rye!' or, 'Have you paid in your proportion of mutton yet?' and he *must* follow up each of these little perquisites, or he would lose the major part of his salary.

"'Monsieur B.!' said the Count, very gravely, 'there is a thirst in the hearts of the people for true religion, and they cannot satisfy it with such teachers.'"*

* Norse Folk, p. 322.

This dissatisfaction with their religious teachers Mr. Brace found almost universal among the middle and upper classes. Such remarks as the following show the state of feeling. "But these men—they have no belief! It is an affair of the pocket. Look at Dr. S., at A. He is known for an infidel, and says openly the Bible is a myth, but still preaches and gets his tithes. Our pastor here is nothing but a genial gentleman. He has his 12,000 riks ($3,000) a-year, and that is all he cares about. He knows no more about the spiritual matters of his people, than if he were a thousand miles away."*

At different periods, however, in the course of the last two centuries, God has raised up men possessed of a zeal for the truth, who have stood like the prophets of old to protest against the ungodliness of priests and people, and to call both alike to the real service of God. And, like the prophets of old, they have uniformly been the subjects of bitter persecution. The Swedish clergy could not brook the earnest rebukes of zealous reformers; and means of persecution will not be long wanting where the spirit of persecution exists. The Council at Upsala had decreed that the Confession of Augsburg was the only recognized religion of Sweden,—that no other form of faith or worship than the Lutheran should be allowed to establish itself

* Norse Folk, p. 318.

in the kingdom,—that the professors of other modes of faith should not be permitted to hold any public meetings in houses or elsewhere; and they threatened confiscation of goods and banishment from the country, to those convicted of holding such meetings, or of speaking injuriously of the religion of the land. With such a decree in full force, the means of crushing all dissent were always at hand.

Almost a century later, Laurentius Ullstadius, a man of piety and zeal, was aroused to effort by the condition of the Church and the people, and he preached with much power and effect in Stockholm. Such a breaking of the long repose of the Swedish church was intolerable. The voice of the reformer must be hushed. The clergy could easily make it appear that the stern condemnation of impiety and formalism which he uttered was speaking injuriously of the religion of the land. He was accused of sacrilege and other crimes, condemned, and sentenced to imprisonment and hard labor for life. For thirty long years, with the faith and patience of the martyrs of old, he endured the rigors of his punishment, until, on the accession of Ulrika Eleonora, a general amnesty was proclaimed and he was liberated. The friends of his youth gone, a stranger in his own land and in his own city, he was sent out thus in his old age a homeless wanderer. He craved the simple boon of being permitted to inhabit till the end of life his prison cell. It was granted;

and there the old servant of God, after a few more years, died, in 1732.

In the year 1723, Eric Tollstadius, a young preacher from the country, was stirred up by the sermon of a dignitary of the Church, in which vital, active piety was grossly abused, to appear as the champion of a spiritual Christianity. On the next Lord's Day, from the same pulpit, he preached to the people of Stockholm the pure Gospel. He was speedily summoned before the Consistory of the church to account for his grave offense. After tedious examinations, he finally appealed to the Diet, by which body he was declared innocent of any ecclesiastical fault. Here the State repressed the persecuting spirit of the Church. Tollstadius, however, was full of fire and zeal; he had been appointed, soon after his first sermon in reply to the bishop, to a church in Stockholm. He was in high fame with the people. "The grace of God which was kindled in him increased day by day. Thousands assembled from all parts of the capital to hear him. The multitude flocked together as if there had been a fire. But indeed there was a fire —oh, a blessed fire—for which many that were inflamed by it, and thus became burning lights, will forever and ever sing praises to the Lamb of God!" Such is the testimony of his biographer, who had the opportunity of knowing him and seeing what he describes. It was not possible for the Church to crush such a man, whom the people, with many of the noblemen, upheld. But they vexed and harassed him with complaints and processes until the day of his death.

But while there have not been wanting, from time to time, men who have been possessed of like spirit with those above mentioned, there has been at no period a deep and wide-spread religious interest. The great mass of the people were left to regard religion as a formal service, for Sundays and holidays.

Among the instruments whom God has raised up for the spread of the Gospel in Sweden, was the Rev. George Scott, a Wesleyan missionary, who was permitted to labor as an English pastor in Stockholm. He commenced his labors in 1830, and met with a very marked success. The year after his first settlement, he began to preach the Gospel in the Swedish tongue, and this drew great crowds to hear him. He mastered the language thoroughly, and used the voice, the press, and the pen, for the promotion of the cause of Christ in Sweden. For twelve years he was instant, in season and out of season, in the prosecution of his work. During the latter part of his sojourn, however, the opposition to him and to his work was assuming a more decided character. In 1838, when an effort was made to raise a more commodious house, in order to accommodate the crowds that were gathering to hear him, he applied to the Government for an Order in Council to secure the property. For ten months, it is said, that the application was resisted by the Consistory of Stockholm, which wished to prohibit him from preaching in the Swedish language. But their efforts were unsuccessful. The king was far more liberal than the clergy.

At length in 1841–42, the spirit of persecution sought other means for the accomplishment of its object. No legal pretext could be found to drive him off; but a series of petty annoyances, increasing in boldness and bitterness, from day to day, might secure the desired result. Their seasons of worship were disturbed by a lewd rabble, like that which finally compelled the Apostle Paul to leave Thessalonica; threatening letters were sent; caricatures flaunted in the shop windows; abuse was heaped on him in the daily press; he was insulted and spit upon when passing to and fro in the streets; a play was got up, in which a character, designed for Mr. Scott, was found guilty of grave crimes, the actor who performed that part having visited the chapel that he might be able to mimic the tones and manner of the preacher.

These means of persecution failing of their object, a riot was the last resort; and this following hard upon the previous hostile demonstrations, produced its ordinary effect. The government could find no legal grounds for proceeding against Mr. Scott; but it was becoming exceedingly troublesome to do battle with a host in defense of one man, and he a foreigner too. The end may be easily predicted. The persistent rabble had it according to their own will, or it may be, according to the will of those who wielded them as tools for the accomplishment of their own ends. The missionary had violated no law, but his services had been the *occasion* of great commotion. Therefore they must be discontinued. This decree was announced in March, 1842. It must be noticed, too, that Mr. Scott did not set up his own ecclesiastical polity in Sweden, that is, did not gather converts into Methodist churches. His offense was seeking to diffuse the knowledge of the gospel, and to bring men to trust in Christ.

The removal of Mr. Scott, nevertheless, did not check the spread of the work in various parts of the kingdom. A great impulse had been given, and the movement did not cease when he was compelled to leave. The Scriptures were eagerly sought after and read by numbers of the people. Readers, or *Lasarne*, as they are called, went to and fro, merely repeating the words of the sacred Scriptures, with a few brief words of explanation, and their labors have been productive of great results. The Lord has remarkably testified to the power of his own word. It is said that persons in some of the more sparsely settled regions of the north will travel many—in one case fifty—miles to attend these services, consisting merely of the reading of the Scriptures, with a few words of running comment and a closing prayer.

In Lapland a remarkable work has been going on, principally through the instrumentality of Lars Levi Laestadius, who was himself first led to understand the love of God in Christ Jesus our Lord, and then to speak of that love to others. The Lapps had been long noted for their drunkenness and lewdness. Under his ministrations the work spread far and wide, and a great moral change has come over the people. Mr. Brace, in his trip to Lapland, found the people cherishing a deep reverence for Laestadius, who died in 1841. He made inquiries in order to ascertain the character of the work that had been going on. One of his conversations with an old Lapland chief is full of interest:

"Is there any fear of demons or evil spirits now among your people?"

"No, except with the poorest persons. We believe. in the redemption through Christ. We do not care for any thing else."

"Is there much drinking in your tribe?"

"No, none. We never drink now. The Spirit of God has been among us."

At the close of the conversation, the old chief turned to Mr. Brace with the inquiry,

"Does the gentleman believe in the baptism of children?"

It appears that there has been, in this work which has been going on, a seeking for what the Scriptures teach, and that among the Lapps there are many who do not find the baptism of infants taught or enjoined in the sacred books.

One of the features which characterize the recent work in Sweden is the spirit of inquiry that has been awakened. The long stagnation of intellect would seem to be breaking up. A writer some years since, in the Edinburgh Review, endeavored to account for the low moral condition of the people of Sweden, by the want of a spirit of inquiry among them. "The power of a priesthood being in the inverse ratio to the spirit of inquiry among the people, such a spirit is checked and discouraged by all means short of active persecution. No offices being open to those who do not take the Sacrament, and offices being numerous, and, in a poor country, much coveted, an unreasoning conformity is produced. Few inquire at the risk of temporal loss."* But now there is a spirit of inquiry aroused. People are now daring to think for themselves. In Sweden, as in every country where a true reformation begins, the people are led to the Scriptures. And in proportion as the reformation is deep and pervading, will it bring every religious doctrine and custom to the test of that all-sufficient rule of faith and practice. In various parts of Sweden the validity of the baptism of infants has been spontaneously questioned. Under the guidance of the Scriptures, many are rejecting

* Ed. Rev. July, 1839.

infant baptism, and seeking the true scriptural baptism—the baptism of believers—as the subsequent narrative will show. It augurs well for the ultimate results of this first popular religious movement in Sweden, that the people are approximating to the true Protestant doctrine: The Bible, the Bible alone the religion of Protestants!

CHAPTER III

THE SWEDISH DIET.

THE Government of Sweden is a limited monarchy. The representative system has been in existence from the earliest ages. The Ricksdag, or Diet, consists of four houses, the nobles, the clergy, the burgers or citizens, and the bonders or peasants.

The House of Nobles consists of three ranks, the counts and barons, knights, and the gentlemen—who, though with no title, are yet by letters-patent ranked among the nobility. The right of representation belongs to the head or senior member of each noble family, and passes by inheritance. The hereditary representative, however, may waive his right in favor of some younger member of his own or of another family. There are about fifteen hundred noble families in the kingdom, though only four or five hundred are represented in the Diet.

The House of Clergy consists of the archbishop and all the bishops, eleven in number—the pastors of the Cathedral at Stockholm, and representatives chosen from the pastors and inferior clergy.

The whole number of the clergy is about twenty-seven hundred, and the total number of members of the house sixty-two.

The House of Burgers or citizens is chosen by all those who are members of guilds or handicrafts in the cities and towns, or who belong to the magistracy. This house has fifty-six members, representing about fourteen thousand voters, more than three times the number represented in the other two houses.

The House of Bonders or peasants comprises one hundred and eleven members, who are the representatives of two and a quarter millions of the population. These peasants are, as a class, rapidly growing in wealth and social influence. They are buying up large quantities of the land owned by the nobles, and are also establishing large and lucrative manufactories of various kinds.

In the Diet, the king or members of any house may make propositions, which are discussed by the other houses, and passed or rejected. Three houses must vote in favor of a bill in order to its final passage; and in case of reform bills, making fundamental changes in the constitution, the whole four houses must concur. And even then the king has an absolute veto. When the houses are divided, two and two, the measure is lost, except in case of financial bills, which are then referred to a special committee of eighteen from each house, whose vote is decisive.

There is a large class of the citizens, numbering about a million of persons, who have no right of representation whatever. Many of these are men of superior intelligence, of wealth, and great social influence. In this class are embraced most of the members of the professions of law and medicine—literary men, the officers of the army and navy, and those persons employed in the coast service, excepting such as belong to one of the four recognized classes. It seems strange that such a body of citizens, so well qualified, apparently, to bear their share in the work of legislation, with honor to themselves and advantage to their country,—should be thus denied the right of representation.

"Such a wretched arrangement," said one of the nobility to Mr. Brace; "the men of property and intelligence shut out, and the clod-breakers voting. There ought to be a law admitting all to suffrage, in some one class, who own land. It is just as stupid in the cities. There is Doctor S., and Professor N.,—you know them,—they cannot vote because they are not burgers, citizens, or members of a guild. It is a slow world here."*

In regard to the working of the cumbersome Diet, there is a widely-spread dissatisfaction. It is so exceedingly difficult to secure the passage of even a simple law. And to expect a thorough reform

* Norse Folk, p. 310.

in legislation seems almost hopeless. The concurrence of all the houses is necessary, and then the king may veto the bill, as he did in 1851, when the whole of the houses passed a bill giving to the House of Bonders the right to elect their own secretary. At present, both president and secretary are appointed by the king.

The nobleman above referred to said: "Many of us are in favor of doing away with the whole system of the four houses, and having a simple parliament of two houses. It takes an age for any liberal bill to get through. The parsons like one thing and the bonders another; and the citizens and nobles are against them both, perhaps. The conservatives with us are the peasants and the clergy. These parsons lead the bonders by the nose."

This system has been a great hindrance in the repeated efforts to secure religious liberty in Sweden. The operation of the unwieldy system may be seen in the case of the Diet of 1856.

At that Diet King Oscar proposed the abrogation of the punishment of banishment for apostacy—that is, for leaving the State Church. He also recommended the suppression of the conventicle acts, which prevent meetings for religious worship except under the direction of the Lutheran clergy.

The suggestions of the king were referred to the Law Committee, which reported to the four houses a bill differing from his propositions. The new bill contained four specifications. The first, instead of abolishing banishment, provided that this should be the only punishment for apostacy, and that the goods of the condemned should not be confiscated as formerly. The second directed that the conventicle laws should be abrogated. The third conceded to Lutherans the right to receive baptism and the Lord's Supper, from the hands of other ministers than those of their own parish church. The fourth allowed those who desired it to use an older, instead of the later, modified form, in administering the ordinances of baptism and the Lord's Supper.

The houses could not agree. The nobles recommitted the first and second, and approved the others. The clergy recommitted the first two, and rejected the third and fourth. The burgers approved of the king's proposal, and rejected the whole of the new bill by a vote of thirty-four to eleven. While the bonders, by a vote of sixty-nine to twenty-one, rejected his proposals. Of course these measures failed. They were not all that was desired, and were open to many objections. Yet it was a step in the right direction.

The action of the Diet was severely commented on by the Swedish press.

"The house of peers has in this question gained fresh laurels of the equivocal kind, of which it has reaped more during this Diet than during any of the more immediate preceding ones. . . . . . The House of Peers formerly piqued themselves in opposing the encroachments of the executive on the liberty of the nation; they now never offer any energetic resistance to the government, but when it in some measure comes forward to promote the interests of public freedom.

"From the priesthood—we mean from their representatives in the Diet—*nothing* is expected. Experience has sufficiently shown, and not least clearly in the present question, that this House is the most obstinate opponent of every advance in liberty, humanity, and civilization. . . .

"The House of Citizens has, in this matter, as in so many others, shown itself the only estate which earnestly and consistently embraces the interests of liberty and humanity.

"In the House of Peasants, most of the speakers were heard to declare that, for their own parts, they entertained no objection to the adoption of the royal bill; but that they considered they ought to yield to the unfounded apprehensions prevalent amongst a part of the population. We cannot but highly disapprove of this idea of representative duty—not to follow our convictions, but to be guided by what we ourselves regard as errors and prejudices."

Great difficulty must be experienced in securing from the House of Clergy their sanction to any act that looks to the curtailment of their power or privileges; and, as they have such influence in the House of Peasants, the wisest measure may be ex pected to fail in a Diet constituted as that of Sweden is. There is, however, hope for the future. The triumphs of liberty of conscience have always been slowly won. A Swedish journalist, in alluding to a previous defeat, like that recorded above, says:

"Although this Parliament thus causes Sweden still to remain under the yoke of oppression of conscience, and with its persecuting laws to stand alone among the Protestant nations, the time has nevertheless come when a conviction of the necessity of change is beginning to prevail. The voice of astonishment, sorrow, and abhorrence, which arises from our Protestant brethren in other lands, on being informed of Sweden's legal way of defending the pure doctrine, will not be in vain, but will, in some measure, help to open the eyes of our people. *Every new instance of persecution is a nail in the coffin of this intolerance, which, as we hope, will before long be ready for burial.*"

The same writer, in referring to the continuance of the old conventicle law, employs strong language, and puts the case in such a light that some, at least, must see the necessity of reform.

"For the next three years it will be regarded in Sweden as a crime—sometimes incurring banishment—that Christians assemble in private houses for edification in their most holy faith. It matters not that all is conducted with decency and propriety, or that every thing which is spoken or sung is entirely orthodox; nay, the very same men who would be regarded as exempt from punishment—harmless for the country and the church, if they were assembled round the card-table or the punch-bowl—are considered criminals and noxious animals if they assemble round the Bible or the Psalm book,"

"We are slow, very slow," is the language of many in Sweden who deplore the persecution which the Diet still upholds and sanctions. Yet the movement goes on. The number of the Baptists is daily increasing, and the ranks of other Separatists from the State church are constantly receiving fresh recruits. Practically it is becoming—if it has not already become—impossible to prevent dissent by punishment, unless in exceptional cases.

The following anecdote was told a few years ago in Stockholm, and at least illustrates the progress of that movement which must virtually repeal a part of the objectionable code.

"What must be done with the Separatists, your Royal Highness?" said one of his ministers to the Crown Prince, now the King of Sweden.

"Banish them all, of course," was the reply.

"An effective remedy, your Royal Highness, but it is now too late to apply it. The whole fleet of Sweden is not sufficient to carry them from our shores."

The self-expatriation of those who prefer freedom of conscience abroad to persecution at home, is also exerting its influence. In an economical view, the continuance of such laws as offer a premium for emigration will be found to be unwise.

In Skania, the agriculturists begin to see the effects of this. Mr. Brace conversed with a wealthy bonder in that part of Sweden, one who was no friend to the Readers.

"Does Herr Socken Skrifvaren* know of much emigration to America from these parts?" said my companion.

"Many hundreds from my village," he answered. "Fools! they could do much better at home. Sweden wants every one now. But it is this cursed Läseri!"

He alluded to the Readers and their doctrine.

"Why, how is that? What have Läsarne to do with it?"

"They turn every one upside down," he answered. "They make disturbances and break the law, and then Herr Resande (Mr. Traveler) knows they must be punished; and so they go to carry on their accursed doings in America."†

This is the testimony of one who was no doubt beginning to feel the economical evil of such large

* That is, Mr. Secretary of the Parish Meeting. Everybody expects his title in Sweden.

† Norse Folk, p. 406.

emigration of some of Sweden's best sons. He was no friend to the Readers, and had not seen the real remedy for such emigration—to proclaim liberty of conscience. Many of those in higher circles have not seen it. They will see it by and by.

Many persons object to the continuance of the House of Clergy, because it gives to such a small proportion of the population such a large share in the legislation. Some object to it because it takes so many of the clergy away from their flocks, where all of their time and attention is needed, and throws them into the arena of political strife. Some few even of the clergy themselves find the expense of their representation to be rather troublesome. One of them who, nevertheless, thought that the House of Clergy ought to be maintained, stated to Mr. Brace, that it cost him twenty-four rix-dollars—six dollars—per month. When the Diet continues in session, as did that of 1856, for sixteen months, the tax becomes heavy to those who have only a limited income. The effect of such protracted absence, on the members of the House of Clergy, and on their flocks, can scarcely fail to be injurious.

At the close of the Diet of 1856,—it ended its session in February, 1858,—the following new Conventicle law was promulgated, which has been regarded as a loss to the cause of religious liberty. The working of this law will be shown in a subsequent portion of this narrative.

"'The gracious statute of the royal majesty,

with regard to the special meetings for devotional exercises, given at the Court of Stockholm, October 26th, 1858.

"'We, Oscar, by the grace of God, etc., make known that we in conjunction with the States of the Kingdom have resolved, while abolishing the royal placard against religious meetings, of January 12th, 1726, and what in other respects has been enacted on this subject, to make the following decree: Members of the Evangelical Lutheran Church shall not be prohibited to meet for social devotional exercises, even though the priests are not present to conduct them. But such meetings may not take place without special permission, during the time when public services of the State Church are being held. Neither shall admittance to such meetings, as cannot be considered family worship, be denied the parish priest, members of church council, or the public authorities in the region; which last-named authorities, in case of any unlawfulness or disorder, are empowered to break up the meeting. Should there stand up any one who is not a priest, or duly authorized by the ecclesiastical laws, to preach at such meetings, and deliver religious discourses which are considered as teaching separation from the Established Church order, or a disregard for the public services of the Established Church, or to the undermining of the sacredness of religion, the Church Council are authorized to forbid him to stand up, in the parish, in the above-named capacity. He that appoints such a meeting, as has been mentioned, at a time when it may not take place, or at such a time opens his house for such meetings, or fails to obey the Church Council's prohibition against exercising the functions of a teacher, shall be compelled to pay a fine of from fifty to three hundred rix-dollars, which sum is to be divided between the accuser and the poor of the parish. If the person fined is not able to pay the fine, the sentence shall be reversed to imprisonment, on the same principles which are valid for changing fines, according to the Chapter of Execution.' "

Mr. Wiberg, in reference to this new decree, uses language, the truth of which subsequent events have unhappily fully verified.

" By the enactment of this law the power to prevent religious meetings is placed much more in the hands of the priests, than heretofore. The parish priest is always the chairman of the Church Council, which consists of only a few members, who are selected by the priest himself. Thus the word of the priest is almost invariably the law by which the others are governed. The priest has only to '*consider*' a discourse as leading to a separation from the State Church, to be empowered to forbid any meetings being held in his parish, to subject them to the above-named fine, or in case of inability to pay, imprisonment."

While we write the Diet is in session. A new

proposal from the king is before the body—a proposal to which there are grave objections. It remains to be seen whether the present Diet will reject this proposal, and go back as the last Diet did. However they may now decide, the people of Sweden will one day have a law to give religious liberty. Who can tell when that day will dawn?

CHAPTER IV.

REV. F. O. NILSSON.

In the summer of 1835, a Swedish sailor might have been seen on the wharves of the City of New York, passing from group to group of recently arrived travelers, whose peculiar dress and language marked them as emigrants from the forest-depths or smiling river banks of old Germany. The sailor would approach one and another with kind aspect and cordial pressure of the hand, thus showing that he sought their welfare. And then he would place in their hands a German tract, which might convey to them the solemn thoughts which he longed, but through ignorance of the language was unable himself to utter.

Thus labored day after day, as Tract Missionary among the German emigrants, Fred. Olaus Nilsson. He had, during the preceding year, been led to the Saviour, and it was now his earnest desire to advance in some way the cause of his divine Master. Very few Swedes or Norwegians came at that time to the shores of the New World, and Nilsson felt a longing desire to speak to his own countrymen, and to his kindred, of the unsearchable riches of Christ.

His desires and his convictions of duty grew so strong, that in the autumn of 1839 he left New York, and went over to his native country in a Swedish vessel. He was strengthened in his conviction that he was in the path of duty, when he found that the blessing of God accompanied his efforts among the crew of the vessel. Several of them, during the voyage, sought and found the Saviour.

Once more at home in his native parish, in the district of Halland, he commenced preaching Christ from house to house among his relatives and friends. Soon the neighbors, and then those from a considerable distance, came to hear the words of eternal life. The work grew on Nilsson's hands, and in a short time the Christian sailor was engaged day and night in preaching Jesus and Him crucified to eager, anxious listeners. He went from village to village, from parish to parish, and, by the blessing of God on his labors, very many souls during the winter of 1839–40, were awakened, and many found peace in believing on Jesus.

In the Spring of 1842, Nilsson was appointed as colporteur among the seamen at Gothenburg, under the direction of the American Seaman's Friend Society. His summers were spent in Gothenburg, but in the winter season he made missionary excursions into the neighboring districts of Bohus, Elfsburg, Skaraburg, and Halland.

While thus laboring for the good of others, his own mind was not entirely at peace. Perplexing questions had arisen. The diligent study of the Scriptures had caused him to doubt the propriety of some things which he had hitherto received unhesitatingly.

Was it right to admit unconverted persons to the Lord's Supper? Was it right for a believer to hold communion and church fellowship with an unbeliever? Was it right for the Church of God to be under the rule of the State? And, lastly, was it right to make the sprinkling of unconscious infants take the place of the baptism of believers.

It was in the year 1845 that Nilsson was first led to search the Scriptures on the subject of baptism. A young Swedish sailor came to Gothenburg. He, like Nilsson, had, while sojourning in America, been baptized in New York, by Rev. Ira R. Steward, pastor of the Mariner's Church. With this Christian brother Nilsson held many interesting conversations on religious subjects. From Hamburg, whither Capt. Shrœder went to join his ship, he wrote to Nilsson, and in his letter he for the first time alluded to the subject of baptism, saying:

"You ought to search the New Testament on the subject of baptism, because it is a subject of greater importance than you have hitherto thought."

These words made a deep impression on Nilsson's mind. He read with much interest the tracts on Baptism which accompanied the letter. Above all, he took heed to the brotherly admonition to "Search the Scriptures."

He went through the New Testament, carefully noting all the passages that speak of baptism, and to his astonishment, he found nowhere that support for infant sprinkling which he had been accustomed to suppose was to be found there. This discovery startled him, and filled him with anxiety. He turned to the writings of Luther, in whom he had ever placed great confidence. But he found that, on this subject, the great Reformer built his arguments on a sandy foundation. They rested not on the sure Word of God. Other Pedobaptist authors he consulted with a similar result.

From books he turned to esteemed friends. He sought the counsel of a learned and pious Lutheran minister, whom he highly respected, and they held frequent and long conversations on the subject.

The result of all this study, research, mental conflict and earnest prayer, was such as, with God's blessing on sincere efforts to know His will, might justly have been expected. Nilsson found that infant sprinkling was nowhere enjoined of God, and the path of duty was plain before him. He must arise and be baptized.

In Sweden there was no one to be found to administer the ordinance. He therefore went to Hamburg in July, 1847.

After some weeks spent in studying the doctrines, articles of faith, and constitution of the Baptist Church in that city, he offered himself as a candidate for baptism. On the 1st of August in that year, he was baptized by Rev. J. G. Oncken, in the river Elbe.

The question now arose, Should he and his wife (who had shared in his conflicts and had arrived at the same conviction as he had) seek in America a home where, unmolested, they might worship God according to the dictates of their conscience,—or should they remain in Sweden, and among their countrymen and former friends bear witness to the truth? They sought guidance from God in earnest prayer, and finally determined to remain in Sweden and confess the truth, whatever might be the consequences to themselves.

Nilsson was fully aware how Baptist, or *Anabaptist* views (as they termed them) would be regarded by his countrymen, and even by his former Christian friends; but trusting in God he went onward. He met, as he had expected, with much opposition. His views of the truth as regarded baptism were met by some with horror, and many whom he regarded as his spiritual children withdrew from him entirely. This was a sore trial. Some, however, were convinced, as he had been, of the necessity of believers' baptism, and were desirous to receive the ordinance.

The church at Hamburg sent Rev. A. P. Fœrster, who, on Sept. 21st, 1848, baptized the wife of Nilsson, two of his brothers and two other believers, in the Cattegat, near Gothenburg. That same night the first Baptist church in Sweden, consisting of six members, was organized in the house of B. N. Nilsson, in the parish of Landa, district of Halland.

Scarcely more than ten years have passed away since that little company of baptized believers banded themselves together in the name of the Lord; and now, in the statistics of the Baptist Churches of Sweden for the year 1859, we find that they number 102 churches, and that the sum total of their membership is 4548. Well may we exclaim, What hath God wrought! Though persecution hath raged, and the rulers have taken counsel together, yet the Word of the Lord has grown mightily and prevailed.

In the spring of 1849, Nilsson went to Hamburg to be ordained. He was ordained by prayer and the laying on of hands by Revs. J. G. Oncken, J. Köbner, and Schauffler, May 6th, 1849, in the meeting-house of the Baptist Church in Hamburg. He returned to Sweden, and continued his labors in the Redeemer's cause, sustained by the Baptist Mariners' Church, New York. But he was not long permitted to proceed unmolested. Several of the members of the church had been brought up before the parish priests and their vestries, and severely threatened, and now Nilsson himself was summoned to appear, July 4th, 1849, before the Consistory of Gothenburg.

After a trial which lasted about two hours, Nilsson was found guilty of having left the true church, and of having maliciously enticed others into heresy. After being admonished to return to the State Church, and warned that in case he continued in heresy the laws would be put in force against him, Nilsson was suffered to depart. The remainder of the year he was unmolested by the civil power, and continued unceasingly engaged in his Master's work.

The priests, however, in many places, commenced preaching against the Baptists, and inflaming the minds of the people. Mobs would often collect around the house in which Nilsson and his little flock were assembled for worship, smashing the windows, breaking in the doors, and assailing the worshipers with stones and other missiles. Besides these personal outrages, persecutions in other forms came thick and fast upon these poor, despised followers of Jesus. Friends and neighbors, and, in some instances, near relatives disowned them, and refused to hold any further intercourse with them. Employers withheld their patronage; and in very many instances the day-laborer, or the weaver, who dared to join himself to the despised Baptists, found himself suddenly turned out of employment, and cut off from the means of earning his daily bread. Much suffering ensued, yet these persecuted ones continued stedfast; and wherever Nilsson went preaching the word, eager listeners assembled to hear him.

On January 1st, 1850, Nilsson was at the house of one of the members of the church, in the District of Elfsburg. A little band were assembled together for prayer and conference. During the day-time they had stationed sentinels to give warning of approaching danger. Having been unmolested during the day, they felt secure when evening drew on, and the sentinels left their posts and joined the little company inside the house. Nilsson was engaged in preaching, when suddenly a loud knocking was heard at the door. On opening it, they found that the house was surrounded by a number of men armed with clubs, pistols, old rusty swords, sticks, and muskets. They were led on by a deputy sheriff, who, after requiring Nilsson to give his name, caused him to be seized and dragged out of the house. The tears and entreaties of his friends were responded to by blows and curses. Nilsson was thrown into a sleigh, and hurried off to the village tavern. At the door of this tavern he was left for a considerable time, exposed to the insults and outrages of the infuriated mob, while his keepers sat within the house, drinking brandy. At last he was taken before the sheriff, who, after threatening and cursing him, committed him to the county jail. The dreary sleigh-ride was resumed, and soon after midnight Nilsson was lodged in a miserable cell. A heap of filthy straw thrown on the stone floor was his only bed. In this wretched abode he was kept in close confinement for six days. No one, not even his wife, was allowed to visit him, nor was he permitted to write to any one.

During the night of January 7th, Nilsson was transferred to Gothenburg, about forty miles distant. Here he was lodged in the district prison, and locked up in a room with eight criminals. Before entering the prison, Nilsson had been permitted, through the humanity of his keeper, to see his wife, and hold converse with her for a few moments. She accompanied him to the threshold; she saw the opening and closing again of the heavy prison gates; she heard the grating of the ponderous bars and bolts that severed her from her husband, and, overwhelmed with grief, she rushed out into the street, weeping and wringing her hands. A friend who recognized her, accosted her with words of kindness and sympathy. She confided to him her sad tale, and he advised her to go direct to the Governor, and relate the facts to him. The Governor granted to Mrs. Nilsson a written order for her husband's release from his unjust and harsh imprisonment. She hastened with it to the jail, and soon his prison doors were opened, and to his surprise and joy he found that he was free.

The respite from persecution was, however, very

brief. About a month later (Feb. 11th) Nilsson received a written summons to appear before the Gotha High Court of Justice, held at Jonköping, to answer to the charges of having adopted and disseminated erroneous sentiments and practices. In a few days he obeyed the summons, making, on his way thither, a wide missionary excursion for the purpose of visiting and strengthening his brethren. Nilsson remained ten days at Jonköping, and appeared twice before the High Court, on the 8th and again on the 11th March. On both occasions the great hall of justice was crowded, and many of the spectators shed tears—so great was the interest excited by this cruel and unrighteous persecution.

Many also manifested a desire to hear more of this way, everywhere spoken against. Nilsson repeatedly addressed large assemblies in his Master's name. On the last Lord's Day of his stay at Jonköping, the numbers that came to hear him were so great, that many remained outside in the street, all listening with earnest attention.

A few days after he had left Jonköping, the minutes of his trial were printed in pamphlet form, and thousands of copies were scattered through the land. It appeared also, with various comments, in most of the leading journals of Sweden. The means used to suppress the preaching of the Word tended rather to its furtherance. In the words of Nilsson:

"From this day the Baptists and their doctrines were no longer confined to an obscure corner of the land, and to a few poor despised laborers. The truth was with trumpet voices proclaimed on the house tops, and the sound thereof re-echoed from cottage to palace, throughout the length and breadth of the land. Thus my appearance before the High Court at Jonköping was the public introduction of Baptist principles into Sweden. Let now the poor sailor be banished from the realm! What matters that! The truths that by his trial have been disseminated in Sweden can never be banished. Soli Deo gloria!"

The sentence of banishment pronounced against Nilsson by the High Court of Justice, was read to him April 29th. Permission being granted to appeal to the king, Nilsson went to Stockholm in the latter part of May. He lodged an appeal in the proper office, and had also a personal interview with King Oscar.

During his stay in Stockholm, Nilsson became acquainted with several pious and evangelical Christians, who had become dissatisfied with the State Church, and were considering the subject of baptism. From them he experienced much Christian sympathy.

Nilsson availed himself of every delay which the law afforded him, in the form of appeals and petitions, not from any hope that his sentence would be reversed, but in order to lengthen out the period of his stay in his native country. He sought to improve this interval by encouraging and exhorting his little flock, who looked forward with sadness and anxiety to the approaching separation.

The period, however, at length arrived when the last petition was rejected, the last warning to leave the country was sounded in his ears. On July 4th, 1851, Nilsson and his wife took leave of their weeping friends, and departed for Copenhagen. They left behind them in Sweden fifty-six baptized believers scattered in different districts. The oversight of this scattered flock was entrusted to Bernhardt N. Nilsson, (brother to Frederic), who is now pastor of the church in Torpa.

Nilsson continued nearly two years with the church in Copenhagen, filling the office of pastor during the last year of his stay. In the spring of 1853, he was urgently solicited by some of the members of the Baptist Church in Sweden to accompany them to the United States. The storm of persecution continued to rage, and a little band of from twenty to thirty believers determined to seek in the New World the privilege denied them in their own land, "freedom to worship God." Nilsson consented to accompany them, and in June, 1853, he and his little flock landed in New York.

Baptists in Sweden.

REV. ANDREAS WIBERG.

CHAPTER V.

REV. ANDREAS WIBERG.

THE period of Nilsson's ministry to the church in Copenhagen, brief through it was, was marked by an incident of no small importance in the history of the progress of Baptist principles in Sweden.

In the month of July, 1852, a Swedish vessel, bound for New York, was detained for two days at Copenhagen, waiting for a favorable wind. Among the passengers was one who, immediately on landing, sought out the residence of the pastor of the Baptist Church, whom he knew by correspondence, though they had never met. The object of the visitor was soon made known. In the language of a disciple in the early days of the Church, he said: "See, here is water, what doth hinder me to be baptized?" The little church in Copenhagen was immediately called together, and listened with deep interest to the candidate's recital of his Christian experience. He was gladly received by the church. That same evening, (July 23d) at eleven o'clock, the little band of baptized believers assembled on the sea-shore to witness the baptism of Andreas Wiberg in the waters of the Baltic.

It was a happy hour for the little church, though perhaps not many there felt the full importance of the act, and the bearing which, in God's providence, it was destined to have on the advancement of the Redeemer's cause in Sweden. Their pastor, however, the devoted Nilsson, who had labored, and prayed, and suffered in that land for the cause of Christ, was greatly encouraged; he felt as if the set time to favor Zion was now come, and he trusted that, by God's blessing, Mr. Wiberg might do very much for the spread of truth and righteousness in Sweden.

A brief sketch of Mr. Wiberg's early life, and of the trials and anxieties of his latter years, will show how God had been gradually but surely fitting him for the post he was destined to fill.

He was born in the year 1816, near Hudiksvall, a small town situated at the head of a deep bay, in Helsingland, in the northeastern part of Sweden. His parents were peasants. A circumstance which occurred when he was fourteen years of age, first awakened his anxiety for the salvation of his soul. He was in imminent danger of drowning, and was saved from death by what seemed almost a miracle. His heart was impressed with gratitude to God for this mercy, and the near view of death caused him to think seriously of his eternal interest. He began reading the Bible, and other religious books. Among the latter was Bunyan's "Holy War," which made a deep impression on his mind.

Mr. Wiberg was at this time engaged in a store in Hudiksvall, but his newly-received religious impressions gave him a desire to be useful in promoting the interests of the kingdom of God. He resolved to study, and for this purpose he went to reside with a pious clergyman in the country. Here his religious impressions were strengthened. But after the lapse of a year he left his pious instructor and placed himself under the tuition of one more learned, but wholly destitute of piety. Under this evil influence, while he made progress in learning, he soon lost all his seriousness.

In 1835 he entered the University of Upsala. Here he studied four years for the degree of Master of Arts. He supported himself while pursuing his studies by teaching, as private tutor, in several families in the town. Though he studied with diligence, the motive which had first prompted him to enter on a course of study was now gone. His ardent desire to serve God had disappeared, and he had even become an unbeliever. Of the state of his feelings at this period his own testimony is,

"This I can say from my own experience, that it is a most unhappy thing to be an infidel."

But at this, the darkest period in his history, relief was nigh. A pious friend came to his room to remonstrate with him on his infidel sentiments, and, among other things, he uttered the solemn words of the Apostle,

"It is a fearful thing to fall into the hands of the living God."

These words pierced as an arrow to his heart.

He determined henceforth to cast aside his infidelity, that "refuge of lies." He fell on his knees, and with tears sought "the living God." But, though his conscience was awakened, he had not yet learned to seek God through Him who is "the Way, the Truth, and the Life." For three long years he continued under the bondage of the law, striving in vain to work out a righteousness of his own, and becoming more and more acquainted with the power of sin and the evils of his own heart. He read much in the German writers of the mystical school, and his perplexities and distress increased till he was brought almost to despair. At length, in his own words,

"By means of a German writer, John Arndt, and through the riches of Divine grace, I was enabled to look upon Him who was lifted up on the Cross for my sins, as the Israelites looked upon the brazen serpent in the wilderness, and I was healed. I believed on Him who justifieth the ungodly; and being justified by faith, I had peace with God through our Lord Jesus Christ."

In the spring of the following year, 1843, Mr. Wiberg became a priest in the State Church of Sweden. He was at first sent from one parish to another to assist aged pastors. He preached with much earnestness and zeal, and the blessing of the Lord accompanied his labors. But soon he began to have doubts respecting the propriety of admitting unconverted persons to the Lord's Supper. This is a general practice in the Lutheran Church in Sweden, where attendance at the Communion table, at least once a year, is necessary, in order to avoid incurring certain legal disabilities. Very few of the ministers of the State Church appear to have had, at that time, any scruples on the subject. All, whether ministers or private Christians, who dared to entertain such scruples, were stigmatized as Separatists and Lasäre, and were the objects of scorn and obloquy.

These conscientious scruples caused Mr. Wiberg much anxiety respecting the course which he ought to pursue, and, as his health had been much impaired by over-exertion in preaching, he resolved to ask permission of the Consistory of Upsala to suspend his labors for a season. This permission was granted, and during the two years he was engaged in the translating and publishing some of Luther's works, and also in editing a paper called "The Evangelist."

There were at this time, in the North of Sweden, a number of pious Christians who had left the State Church, owing to scruples similar to those entertained by Mr. Wiberg. Being acquainted with his views, and having confidence in him as a truly Evangelical minister, they applied to him to separate formally from the State Church, and to become their pastor. He had not yet become fully convinced that it was his duty to take this decisive step, but his correspondence with these Christians caused him to be twice summoned before the Consistory of Upsala. The first time he was suspended for three months, on the charge of not being in subjection to the Church. The second time, his accuser, a dean of his native place, Hudiksvall, urged his banishment from the kingdom, because he had written an apology for the Christians in the North, who were at this time suffering persecution on account of their separation from the Church. Mr. Wiberg now appealed from the ecclesiastical to the civil tribunal; but, while the cause was pending, his accuser, a learned man, and advanced in life, put an end to his days by hanging himself. No other person appeared to urge on the suit, and thus he was freed for the time from persecution.

At this period a few minds in Stockholm began to be interested in the subject of baptism. A Swedish gentleman, Mr. P. J., who was a resident of Hull, in Yorkshire, England, made a visit to his native country in 1849. He was a Baptist, and his conversations on the subject of baptism with some of his friends interested them deeply. The year following sentence of banishment was pronounced against Mr. Nilsson, who, as we have seen, made a brief visit to Stockholm for the purpose of appealing to king Oscar. All these circumstances contributed to draw the attention of Christians more strongly to the subject. Mr. Wiberg, who was in constant intercourse with these Christian friends strongly opposed their views on baptism. He was strongly attached to the writings and doctrines of Luther, and could not consent to consider him in error on any point.

In the spring of 1851 he visited Hamburg. A friend, Mr. D. Forssell, was going thither on business, and requested Mr. Wiberg to accompany him as interpreter of the German language. While in Hamburg he visited the Baptist Church in that city, and became acquainted with Rev. J. G. Oncken and Rev. J. Köbner. The spirituality and earnest piety of this church were noticed by Mr. Wiberg with heartfelt pleasure. Its constitution and discipline appeared to him to be formed on the apostolic model. But to the views of baptism which they held he could not assent, and he had several discussions with his Baptist friends without being shaken in his own views.

On his departure from Hamburg Mr. Köbner gave him several tracts on baptism, among which was a copy of the German translation of Pengilly's Scripture Guide to Baptism, published by the AMERICAN BAPTIST PUBLICATION SOCIETY. This he read on his return to Sweden, and when he saw the exposition which Pengilly gives of 1 Cor. vii. 14, his former confidence in infant baptism began to be shaken. To use his own words:

"The first doubts about the divine origin of infant baptism were aroused in contemplating this text. (1 Cor. vii. 14.) He had previously been of opinion that, though there could not be found any distinct example in the New Testament, as an evidence in favor of infant baptism, yet it might be possible that it had an apostolic origin, as no distinct example could be found against such a supposition. But from this passage he saw that if infant baptism had been introduced by the Apostle into the Corinthian Church, he would not, under any circumstances, have questioned whether the children might not have been 'unclean,' because baptism would have made them 'holy.' "*

He now commenced reading with eager interest Hinton's "History of Baptism." He was not yet fully persuaded, but he perceived and understood enough to make him shrink from the thought of sprinkling unconscious infants.

The Christians in the north were awaiting his decision on the question of becoming their pastor. Before the journey to Hamburg, he was on the point of complying with their request. But now it became necessary to write to them of his change of views, and to tell them that he could not sprinkle their children, because he thought it not in accordance with the teachings of Scripture. They were shocked and amazed. In their perplexity they wrote to a clergyman in Finland, a learned man, and one whom they highly esteemed. The reply of their friend was couched in terms of bitter denunciation, and Mr. Wiberg was made to appear

* Christian Baptism: By Rev. A. Wiberg, issued by the American Baptist Publication Society.

in the eyes of his former friends as a noxious heretic and an apostate, not only from the Lutheran faith, but from the Lord Jesus Christ. This was a severe trial. His letters produced but little effect on their minds, as they were counteracted by the letters which they received from Finland.

At last he promised them to write a book, which might prove a complete reply to the false statements and calumnies of which he was the object.

From Mr. Nilsson, with whom he was in correspondence, Mr. Wiberg obtained Dr. Carson's valuable work, "Baptism in its Mode and Subjects." This he studied carefully, comparing all the arguments and statements with the New Testament in the original Greek.

While engaged on this work, Mr. Wiberg was attacked by a severe illness, which continued for three months. When he began slowly to recover strength, he applied himself to completing his book. He also held meetings and preached the gospel. At these meetings some were led to inquire what they should do to be saved, and found peace in believing on Christ. But the arm of the law interposed, and the Governor of Stockholm prohibited these meetings. An influential newspaper, however, advocated their cause, and they were again permitted to assemble together.

Mr. Wiberg's health still continued very infirm, and the physician advised a sea voyage as the best means of restoring his strength. At this time an opportunity presented itself to him of obtaining a free passage to the United States. He gladly availed himself of this. He earnestly desired to be baptized, and it was his hope that in America this desire might be fulfilled. But, as we have already seen, he was permitted, in the providence of God, to receive baptism at Copenhagen, a few days after leaving the shores of Sweden.

CHAPTER VI.

MR. WIBERG IN AMERICA.

THE hand of Providence, which had brought Mr. Wiberg thus far, was by this means conducting to results which he had little anticipated on leaving his native land. On his arrival in this country he was at once brought into connection with those whose views and principles accorded with his own, and by his intercourse with the Baptists of the United States, their attention was drawn to the opening for Christian effort, presented in Sweden.

Mr. Wiberg first landed in New York, where he was cordially received by the Mariners' Church in that city, to which he had a letter of introduction from Mr. Nilsson. Here he labored for a time as Colporteur of the AMERICAN BAPTIST PUBLICATION SOCIETY, among seamen, in connection with the Mariners' Church. He subsequently visited Philadelphia, where he remained for a considerable time, engaged in preparing books and tracts in Swedish, under the direction of this same Society.

Meanwhile the work of God was going on in Sweden. The book on Baptism, which Mr. Wiberg had completed and left for publication before sailing for the United States, was circulating in different parts of the country, and arousing an earnest spirit of inquiry. The letters from that country, which told of the progress of the work and of the persecution endured by those who ventured to worship God according to the dictates of their conscience, awakened a deep and prayerful sympathy in the hearts of Baptists in America.

We subjoin a few extracts from some of these letters. The first are taken from a letter written by Mr. Forssell, a Christian merchant in Stockholm, who has endured much and sacrificed much for the cause of Christ:

STOCKHOLM, Jan. 18, 1854.

"I have to-day received a letter from the Parish of Mora, in Dalarna, from F., a book-keeper. We traveled through this parish when we were at Orsa, and were summoned before the court last summer. This man was then very much afraid, fearing the world. But by our meeting him and the friends there, a great change has taken place. They now assemble regularly every Sunday to hear the word of God, and even in the week-days. F. has been in great measure freed from the fear of man, and he now confesses the Lord Jesus with great courage. . . . Through brother Palmquist, I hear that the brethren in America are willing to make sacrifices for Sweden, and that they would be willing to sustain Colporteurs or Home Missionaries, if only they had proper subjects." He then names several among them some who have since been eminently successful in preaching the Gospel. He adds:

"It seems that the Lord is preparing for Himself instrumentalities in a very short time, and that He destines the Baptists to break down the strong wall with which the State Church has surrounded herself. . . . . I believe the instrumentalities are here, but means are wanting. Pray, therefore, the American friends not to be wearied in showing love toward the poor Christians in Sweden."

The next letter, from which we make extracts, was written a year later, by one of those whom Mr. Forssell mentioned as able and anxious to labor for the salvation of souls in Sweden, Rev. P. F. Hejdenberg. He went to Hamburg in the spring of 1854, and was there baptized by Rev. J. G. Oncken, and ordained a minister of the Gospel.*

This letter is dated "January 20th, 1855, from the Cell-prison of the District of Stockholm," into which he had been thrown for the *crime* of preaching salvation through Christ, and baptizing those who believed on His name. It will be noticed with what earnest entreaty he asks the people of God to pray for him.

"My dear brethren:—My design in these lines is to ask you to pray for me and cry to the Lord, that

* See page 125.

He may be with me and guide me, as He has promised, in the right way, for His name's sake. You know very well that I am considered as a seducer and rebel, one who teaches against the temple, against the law, and against the power. And you may soon find that it is not just that such a man should live. I therefore most earnestly ask those who know Jesus, and have the wings of prayer, to fly to the throne of the Father and pray for me. . . . . . Do not forget to hold prayers and intercession for me and all. Remember that God has promised to hear prayer. And perhaps the salvation of thousands will depend on it. Think what intolerance!—One must rise from bed, leave wife and children, and immediately follow to prison, for no other reason than, as you know, that I have denied 'the true evangelical doctrine' by preaching Jesus Christ and Him crucified, that He alone is the way to heaven and salvation, and the only Foundation—because I teach "he that believes and is baptized shall be saved"—and because I have received the Lord's Supper together with believers only, and *not with the world,* which is the synagogue of Satan and the enemy of God. This is my crime. . . . . What does Christ say: 'My kingdom is not of this world.' Think now, the whole world is received into the kingdom of Christ! Is it reasonable? Should we not awake and look around us for the track of the truth? . . . . Oh that we were wise, and put it to our hearts, and did not suffer ourselves to be kept under the statutes of the world—the commandments of men—but instead of this followed our conscience—followed Christ even to the prison vault. We then should realize what the Spirit and the Word are able to do. . . . I ask still once more—pray for me—pray for my wife, who is a sister, that she may not be overwhelmed by too much distress. Dear friends, let us hold fast the profession of our faith. Let us go forth without the camp, bearing the reproach. The grace of our Lord Jesus Christ and the love of God our Father be with you all, wishes and prays your brother,

P. F. Hejdenberg."

The letter from which the above extracts are made, was read at the meeting of the American Baptist Publication Society, at Chicago, Illinois, in May, 1855. It was listened to with deep interest and heartfelt sympathy. All felt that it was the time to put forth efforts to assist those who were thus suffering and laboring in the cause of Christ.

At this meeting in Chicago the Committee on Foreign Colportage and Publication made the Report from which the following extract is taken :

"From the Report of the Board, and papers therewith submitted, your Committee have learned the following facts. For a considerable period there has been a most interesting work of grace in progress in Sweden. Within the past year, one of the subjects of this work, a dissenter from the Established Church, and a minister of the gospel, has received the ordinance of baptism in the city of Hamburg, and he in turn has administered the ordinance to a very large number in his native land. The work is still progressing, but the disciples are subjected to grievous and sore trials. 'Freedom to worship God,' in the sense in which we speak of it in this country, is a blessing not enjoyed in Sweden. The spirit of persecution reigns there, and the strong arm of the civil law is brought to bear against the public preaching of the gospel among all dissenters from the Established Church. According to very recent intelligence, the ministering brother to whom we have just referred, is now in prison for no other crime than preaching the gospel, not according to the law; and like the primitive Christians, the disciples there are praying for his deliverance, and sending him their contributions for the support of himself and family. How long this persecution will continue, or to what results it will lead, your Committee will not venture to suggest. They think, however, that it will be apparent to all that the prosecution of this work of evangelism, by the direct preaching of the gospel, must meet with very serious obstacles for a considerable time yet to come.

"But while the preaching of the gospel to assemblies convened for the purpose is thus contravened by the law in Sweden, entire freedom is given to the press. Books and tracts, containing the same doctrines we preach, may be published and circulated there, with none daring to hinder. Moreover, your Committee have learned that several works, more or less extensive, have already been published under the auspices of this Society, suited to the exigencies of the case, and that several laborers are ready to engage in the distribution of these works among the people. The Rev. Andreas Wiberg, now in this country, an accomplished scholar and devoted Christian, the author of a work of rare ability, published in the Swedish language by this Society during the past year, is now ready to return to his fatherland, and it is believed that he is eminently qualified to guide and comfort and instruct his brethren there in these days of trial and persecution.

With these facts before them, your Committee have felt that a system of colportage for Sweden should be devised by this Society at the earliest practicable moment. It has appeared to them that here is a field prepared of the Lord for just such a work as this Society is appointed to accomplish. While a strictly missionary organization might encounter serious opposition, and its laborers be subjected to fines and imprisonment, if not banishment from the country, before this Society there is set an open door, and God, in his gracious providence, seems inviting us to enter it.

"Your Committee would therefore recommend that the Board be requested early to consider the propriety of establishing a system of Colportage in Sweden.

"In behalf of the Committee,
"D. B. Cheney, *Chairman.*"

Before speaking of the manner in which this recommendation of the Committee was carried out, we will give some extracts from another letter from Sweden, written at this period. They show the progress of the work and the earnest desire for the return of Mr. Wiberg to Sweden.

"Stockholm, Jan. 6, 1855.

"Dear Brother Wiberg:—Your labor here is very important. They are writing and speaking against the Baptists all over the land. Your book on Baptism, lately published in America, is mentioned in the newspapers, and the people warned not to read it when it comes. Our adversaries are anxious to get it beforehand, in order to refute it before we can get hold of it. This shows how zealous they are against us. As soon as you return, I hope you will publish a religious paper, in which you may, with the words of truth, enlighten the gainsayers, and make our brethren more stedfast in the faith. For that purpose, I myself am determined to give seven hundred and fifty rix-dollars as soon as you arrive. Now my entreaty is that you would write immediately, and let us know how soon you will come. Take very good care of your health, that you may not get sick. Come soon, dear brother, for many are longing for you.

"I am sorry to say that some twenty of the brethren in and about Norrköping have turned back to the State Church. This has been for us very painful indeed, and it has frightened some from uniting with us. In Dalarna, however, the Baptists have increased to nearly three hundred. And in Norrland many are waiting for baptism. You are needed here far more than in America. For in America are organized congregations, but here it is not so. And besides that, dear brother, we are only a few laymen against a great number of learned priests, and the whole State Church. You know very well how it is.

"Fifteen of our brethren and sisters in Dalarna have lately been imprisoned for a certain time on bread and water, as a punishment for taking the Lord's Supper out of the State Church. I have just heard that they were very happy in prison. They were liberated on the week of Christmas. Brother Hejdenberg is now sentenced to twenty-eight days on bread and water for having held meetings and preached the Gospel in more than twenty places. It will be some time yet before his doom will be sentenced in the High Court. His financial circumstances will not permit him to purchase his freedom, nor would he do it if he could.

Lord God, strengthen him that he may bear with submission the chastisement!

"Dear brother, once more I would say, *come soon to Sweden;* and this pressing desire is not mine only, but it is the desire of us all. May the Lord incline your heart to come soon, and may you have a happy voyage. All the brethren and sisters salute you.—Yours, in Christ,

DAVID FORSSELL."

These earnest desires of the brethren in Sweden were fulfilled, and the recommendation of the Committee in Chicago carried out by the appointment of Mr. Wiberg to the post of Missionary Colporteur in Sweden. It may here be stated, that in the spring of the year Mr. Wiberg made an application to the Committee of the Missionary Union, requesting appointment as Missionary to Sweden. To this application the Corresponding Secretary replied that, on account of the financial condition of the Union, "it would be impossible to entertain the question of planting a new mission in any country."

Mr. Wiberg had, as we have seen, been engaged for a considerable time in preparing the necessary books and tracts for circulation in that country. After his appointment, he spent a few weeks in visiting the churches in behalf of his mission. On the 23d of August, public services were held in connection with his departure to his field of labor. An account of this meeting was widely published in our denominational papers, from one of which we copy the following particulars:

"The services connected with the designation of the Rev. ANDREAS WIBERG, as Superintendent of Missionary Colportage in his native country, the kingdom of Sweden, were held on Thursday evening last, in the Sansom street Baptist Church, Philadelphia. Notwithstanding the evening was stormy, the spacious edifice was crowded. The Rev. Joseph H. Kennard, Chairman of the Board of Managers of the American Baptist Publication Society, under whose auspices Mr. Wiberg returns to Sweden, presided on the occasion.

"In the unavoidable absence from the city of the Corresponding Secretary, the instructions of the Board were delivered to Mr. Wiberg by the Rev. J. Newton Brown, D. D., the Editorial Secretary of the Society. The following is a brief synopsis of the address:

"'This night,' said Dr. Brown, 'the AMERICAN BAPTIST PUBLICATION SOCIETY enters upon a new work—the establishment of a system of Foreign Missionary Colportage in the kingdom of Sweden. We meet to bid farewell to our beloved brother, Rev. Andreas Wiberg, who goes out as the first superintendent and organizer of the system. He is a native of Sweden, a graduate of the University of Upsala, and was for years an esteemed minister of the Lutheran Church in that country.

"'It may be necessary to explain to this audience why we undertake this work—especially as it may seem to some to belong more appropriately to the Foreign Missionary Union of our denomination. The peculiar position of things in Sweden at this time accounts for the procedure, and throws this work into our hands. The Missionary Union is dear to us. But God has opened to us a door in Sweden, which is at present shut against them. *Preaching* is there legally prohibited out of the Established Church under heavy penalties, imprisonment on bread and water for twenty years, or banishment for life.

"'But the press is free—free among a population of three and a half millions who are all able to read—who are now awakened of God to an extraordinary spirit of religious inquiry—who are calling for that light which our tracts and books can diffuse, and which our brethren there are ready to circulate with zeal, courage and prayer. Since the time that Gustavus Wasa threw off the yoke of Denmark and of the Pope, more than three centuries ago, never has there been such a call to evangelical labor as now.

"'Even in regard to preaching and to religious liberty, there is hope. The Constitution of 1809 guarantees to all the people of Sweden full liberty of conscience; and there is a large party of liberal men who are contending for the abolition of the old persecuting laws, which the established clergy

—the most powerful body in the State—are anxious to uphold. It is evidently a period of transition, as well as of proscription.

"'All vital, serious piety, even in the Establishment, has been persecuted, from the time of the German Spencer—more than a century ago—and especially so at its present powerful revival, attended with a large secession from the Establishment, and the adoption of Baptist principles by many. Many of our brethren have suffered from heavy fines and close imprisonment. But they suffer joyfully, and the work of God goes on.

"'This is the state of things which demands the establishment of an Evangelical Baptist Press, and a system of Missionary Colportage in Sweden. A special Providence has brought to our shores and to our city the very man that the position of his native land requires. He came for his health. He has been here three years. He has regained his health, acquired our language, translated and composed works adapted to the exigency, established himself in the esteem and confidence of all who know him, and now, at the urgent call of his Swedish brethren, returns to take charge of this interesting work.

"'It will be expected by the Board of Managers that the Rev. Mr. Wiberg will, immediately upon his arrival at Stockholm, the capital of Sweden, organize a system of Colportage, select and superintend the Colporteurs, form and confirm in the faith the infant churches now rising all over the country, establish and conduct a monthly periodical devoted to the defense of vital piety and religious liberty as understood by the Baptists, and first of all diffused by them throughout the United States, that he will exert himself, in conjunction with other friends, to secure it legally in Sweden by petition and argument, and in case of failure and punishment, to retire just beyond the line of Sweden to the capital of Norway—a place almost equally central for effective operations in Sweden, Norway, and Finland—from which six to eight millions of Scandinavian population can be reached by Colportage and the Press.

"'Having in years past translated the works of Luther and Arndt from the German into his native tongue, he will be expected now to add to them translations from the English, adapted to the wants of these millions. Accustomed to conduct, in former years, an evangelical press, he will be enabled now to add those evangelical views of the ordinances of Christ and the holy constitution of Christian churches, which he has more recently obtained from the study of the New Testament.

"'In a word, every energy is to be consecrated, every available means employed, if like Paul, 'by all means he may save some,' where God is opening before him a wide effectual door, though there be many adversaries.'

"After the instructions had been given, the

prayer of designation was offered by the President of the meeting, and the hand of fellowship was presented by Dr. Dowling. This was affectingly responded to by brother Wiberg, in a few words expressive of his gratitude to God and to his American brethren. He said that he came to this country three years ago a poor stranger, with no idea of making a protracted stay. He might well exclaim, 'What has the Lord done for me!' He felt conscious of his own weakness; and like a little child, who, in order to take its first step, must grasp the hand of its parent, so he could only be sustained by the hand of his heavenly Father. He earnestly implored the prayers of his American brethren and friends to encourage him in his weakness, and to follow him to the field of his labor, and perhaps of persecution and suffering.

"Interesting and appropriate addresses were then made by the Rev. Messrs. Henry Day, of the Broad Street Church; J. W. Smith, of the Spruce Street Church; and Thomas S. Malcom; after which a liberal collection was taken toward the expenses of the voyage.

"Dr. Dowling then united in marriage the Rev. Andreas Wiberg and Miss Caroline Lintemuth, a much-beloved member of the Sansom Street Church, and for several years the teacher of the Infant Department of their Sunday-school."

Of this lady, Dr. Steane, in his "Tour in Sweden,"

remarks: "Mr. Wiberg returned from America endowed with the greatest of all earthly blessings, a pious and affectionate wife." Those of her friends in Philadelphia who knew her best, regarded her as eminently calculated to be a companion and a helpmeet to Mr. Wiberg in the life-work to which he had devoted himself.

Mr. and Mrs. Wiberg sailed on the 8th of September. They arrived in Stockholm on the 7th of November; having spent a few days on the way with the brethren in Hamburg.

CHAPTER VII.

STOCKHOLM.

THE return of Mr. Wiberg was hailed with joy by the church in Stockholm, and the brethren in Dalarna and Helsingland were equally cheered and encouraged by his arrival. Their adversaries also took note of it, and the following passages from the "Watchman" show the state of feeling which they wished to excite:

"Since the principles of the Baptists have been proclaimed among us, especially during the last year, we have seen with sorrow that this new doctrine has gained many adherents in our country. . . . Mr. Wiberg, we perceive, has returned from America as a Baptist teacher, and is living here in the capital. His work, the largest that has been published on the doctrine of the Baptists, has been republished in America, and a large stock has been sent to this country for sale. Smaller works have also been edited by him and Möllersvärd, in order to give their doctrines a wider circulation. While the Baptists are thus busy, it seems to be of the greatest importance that we should redouble our efforts. For our part, we, of course, cannot advise the adoption of coercive measures against the Baptists; but if the guardians and rulers of the Church do not intend to use the strong arm of the law, as prudence dictates, let them not fall into indifference; but remembering their high calling to feed the flock, let them cheerfully seize the two-edged sword of the word. We have said that many good books have been put forth against the Baptists. Let them be widely circulated; let small, popular treatises be multiplied in large editions, and sent abroad among the people, and let the teachers of the Church, on special occasions, explain to the people the doctrine of baptism."

All this has been done. The pulpits have resounded with denunciations of the Baptists. During the years 1854–55, no less than fourteen different treatises against Baptist views were published and widely circulated; and the "coercive measures" which the "Watchman" would not advise, but the use of which he intimates "prudence dictates," have been freely used, and many a Baptist has been made to feel the weight of "the strong arm of the law." In some few instances it has been used successfully. Here and there some faint-hearted ones have shrunk from imprisonment, spoliation, scorn and obloquy, and have returned to the State Church. But the vast majority have held fast the profession of their faith without wavering, and large numbers have been added to the churches. The following pages will show that from Yngsio, in the extreme south of Sweden, up to Lulea, verging toward the Arctic Circle, the preaching of the Baptist colporteurs has been the power of God unto the salvation of many souls.

The church in Stockholm, under the joint pastoral charge of Rev. A. Wiberg and Rev. Charles Möllersvärd, numbered, in 1855, forty-five members; in 1858 its numbers had increased to one hundred and forty-nine. In Stockholm, the meetings of the Baptists have not been disturbed by the authorities. The country districts and regions more remote from the capital have been the chief scenes of persecution.

Very arbitrary measures, however, are sometimes employed, even in Stockholm. About a month before Mr. Wiberg's arrival in Stockholm, the court preacher, Wenshöm, accompanied by police-officers, entered the house of Mr. Forssell, and baptized, by force, his little child of six months old. This is the same spirit which dictated the seizure of the infant child of a Baptist near Strängnas. He had refused to have his child sprinkled; the district sergeant came, and by force took the child to the cathedral, where it was christened with much ceremony. And it recalls the shameful oppression of the earlier days of the Baptists in Sweden, when, in 1850, the authorities came down on two poor families, seized from each their only cow, and sold them at public auction, to pay the district sergeant for carrying off their children to be sprinkled, and to pay the priest his fee. Happily such violence is now checked. In a recent number of the "News of the Churches," we find the following:

"In many cases, heretofore, Baptist parents have had their children taken from them by the policeman, carried to the priest, and forcibly baptized. It has now been ascertained and declared, at the instance of the Consistorium of Upsala, that no law exists warranting this odious and profane practice."

Very shortly after the return of Mr. Wiberg, the organization of the church was completed by the election of officers. The joint pastors of the church held frequent services, preaching several times during the week in a hall, which, although large, was too small for the accommodation of the hearers.

Previous to Mr. Wiberg's arrival, the charge of the church in Stockholm had devolved, in a measure, on Mr. Möllersvärd. This young preacher of the gospel was sent forth and is still sustained by the contributions of the Mariners' Baptist Church, in the city of New York. He was baptized in that city by Rev. Ira R. Steward, pastor of the Mariners' Church. On his return to Sweden, he preached in different parts of Dalarna, Helsingland, and also visited the island of Aland.

On the 1st of January, 1856, Mr. Wiberg issued the first number of a semi-monthly paper, called "The Evangelist," with six hundred subscribers.

It soon reached a circulation of one thousand copies, and in 1858, it had doubled that number. This paper has proved a powerful auxiliary to the preached word, and several have received their first serious impressions from its perusal.

During the summer of this year, the whole charge of the church in Stockholm devolved on Mr. Wiberg, while Mr. Möllersvärd was absent on a missionary tour. During this period he administered the ordinance of baptism for the first time in Sweden. He had hitherto avoided doing it, lest it might subject him to serious persecution, which, in his peculiar position, it was his duty, if possible, to avoid. He had the privilege during the summer of baptizing twenty-four persons, who united with the church in Stockholm.

At this period four of the brethren were set apart to the work of the ministry—Gahm, Forss, Ohssen, and Carlander.

In March of this year, the Missionary Union of Stockholm was formed, for the purpose of sustaining and aiding Colporteurs. This Society is composed mainly of Baptists.

The want of a school, where the colporteurs might more fully qualify themselves for their important work, began now to be deeply felt. In October of this year, a school was formed for this purpose. A well qualified teacher from the north of Sweden was employed to take charge of it for six months, and Rektor Frykstcd and Mr. Wiberg gave lectures on theological subjects three times a week. During this winter, four young men were trained in this school, one of whom was Brother Sven Svenson, of Skänia.*

The hope that liberty of conscience was about to be granted, excited at this time deep and prayerful emotions in the hearts of Baptists in Sweden. King Oscar had declared to the Diet his intention to bring before them a law to this effect. And even Bishop Thomander had expressed himself in favor of granting to Baptists "a patent right to exist, but not to increase."

Mr. Wiberg, in speaking of the hall where their religious meetings were held, writes, "It is too small to contain all who come. If we *should obtain religious liberty*, and be able to raise the means for building a meeting-house, I have no doubt we should soon see it filled." Of this hall we find the following description by Dr. Steane:

"It is situated in one of the narrow streets which constitute the heart of the city. It was formerly used as a public gymnasium; the whole house, however, has been purchased by two of the members of the church, in order that the gymnasium might be used as a chapel. It is plain, but neatly and conveniently fitted up with seats—movable benches with backs to them—and will hold about four hundred persons. Its chief and very obvious want is

* See page. 134.

altitude, the height being only that of an ordinary dwelling-room."*

During the spring and summer of 1857, Mr. Wiberg was disabled from preaching by illness, which for a season confined him entirely to his room. Mr. Möllersvärd being absent on a missionary tour at this period, the congregation for a time diminished. But in August of this year, Rev. G. Palmquist returned from America, and was welcomed with joy. In Mr. Wiberg's diary we find the following:

"Sunday, August 23.—This day, enjoyed the privilege of welcoming to his native land, after an absence of six years, our beloved brother G. Palmquist. May the Lord bless him, and make him a great blessing to his native land. We attended meeting together in the evening, when I introduced him to our congregation as a brother beloved in Christ. He then made some interesting remarks, bearing Christian salutation from the Christians in America to the Christians in Sweden."

The following week Mr. Wiberg set out on a tour in Helsingland, leaving the church in Stockholm under the charge of Mr. Palmquist, who preached for them for five weeks. During this time several were baptized, among whom was his brother, Mr. Peter Palmquist, and his wife. The Sunday-schools were placed under the charge of these two brothers. Mr. G. Palmquist was superintendent of the one in

* Notes of a Tour in Sweden, p. 45.

the city, and Mr. P. Palmquist of the one in the Southern District. Owing to the strong efforts of the priests to prevent the children from attending the Sunday-schools, it has been difficult to sustain them, especially as there was a lack of proper question-books and library books. There were, however, at the close of 1858, eight hundred and sixty children gathered into Sunday-schools in different parts of Sweden.

The following passage from a letter of Mr. Wiberg's, written during this winter, gives a pleasing picture of a working church:

"The brethren of our church go out two and two every Sunday, sometimes several miles beyond Stockholm, and read and expound the Word of God; while the sisters go from house to house distributing tracts and conversing with the impenitent."

From several interesting incidents connected with this tract distribution, we extract the following:

"One of the visitors offered a tract to an aged female, who, observing in her hand the tract entitled 'Look to Jesus,' exclaimed, 'Oh, give me that! It was loaned to me some time ago to read. It led me to Jesus, and has been the means of bringing joy and peace to my soul.' When she received the little book, she kissed it and said, 'This is now mine—the other was borrowed, and with regret I was obliged to return it.' She thanked the giver most gratefully, at the same time kissing her hand repeatedly."

Well may we exclaim with Mr. Wiberg, "O, that Christians everywhere might be led to appreciate more and more this quiet, unobtrusive method of winning souls to Christ." The Publication Society has a list of nearly three hundred most excellent tracts—shall they not be circulated by millions?

In June, 1858, the second Annual Association of the Baptist churches in Sweden was held in Stockholm. It was largely attended by ministers and delegates from the Baptist churches in all parts of the country. Some from other countries were also present: Rev. J. G. Oncken, and J. Köbner, from Germany; Rev. E. Steane, D.D., and Rev. J. H. Hinton, from England; and Mr. Johnson, brother of one of the deacons of the church in Stockholm, but himself for many years a resident of Hull, England.

The meeting of the Evangelical Alliance, which took place about the same time, rendered this a season of peculiar interest to Christians in Stockholm.

Dr. Steane and Mr. Hinton had received, as Secretaries of the Baptist Union of Great Britain and Ireland, an invitation to attend the Association of the Baptist churches in Sweden. They complied with this invitation, and were very cordially welcomed. They attended the meetings of the Association, and also those of the Evangelical Alliance. The notes of their visit, which they published on their return, show that every effort was made to render their stay in Stockholm pleasant and interesting. These notes also mention the interview which Dr. Steane and Mr. Hinton had with the Archbishop of Upsala, and some other persons in authority, to endeavor to obtain liberty of conscience for their brethren in the faith. They were courteously and politely received, with fair words and flattering hopes; but subsequent events have shown that, in this case, as in many others, unwavering hostility may be concealed under the language of fairness and courtesy.

We therefore extract from this little volume, neither the correspondence with the Primate nor the interview with the Royal Chancellor, but the simple narrative of a brief interview with a Dalecarlian peasant, whose honest, heartfelt utterances will, we are assured, be found interesting.

At two o'clock dinner was partaken of by all the delegates to the Association, and the delegates from England were the objects of peculiar attention and interest. An eager group was formed around them.

"Dr. Steane espied a tall, fine figure, a Dalecarlian in his provincial costume, and expressed a desire to speak to him. I have seldom seen a finer expression than in the face of the individual who now came and sat down before us—so much strength and so much sweetness. Dr. Steane inquired how far he had come to be present at the meetings. 'Some three hundred and fifty miles,' was the answer. 'And how have you come?' 'Mostly walking.' This, however, seemed nothing in his estimation; but that these dear English brethren should have come so far to see us, that was a wonder. His eyes glistened at the thought. He would gladly have gone twice as far to see such a sight. 'And are you an elder, or a teacher?' 'I?—oh, no!' he answered; 'I am an ignorant man; I could not write or spell a word if you would give me the whole world. I have only to learn from others, and to speak about the abundant grace of God as experienced by myself.' After a little while he added: 'How I should like to speak to these dear brethren; but here I am sitting like a poor mute.' Certainly, however, this was not the case,—his eyes spoke volumes. Dr. Steane said to him, 'Babel divided us, but Pentecost again united us. There is really only one language among the hearts of those who love the Lord Jesus Christ.' 'Yes,' said the Dalecarlian, 'and some time there will be only one language for their lips, too, and one song, the song of the Lamb.' His expression was very beautiful, and it seemed to make the brightest of thoughts brighter still, by bringing it out at the very moment when hearts were at a loss to express to each other that very love which will be the essence of the song to be sung in heaven, when all the differences of this world shall have passed away.

"Subsequent conversation with him elicited the

fact that he was a recent and remarkable example of the power of Divine grace. A young girl, he told us, in the farm service, first spoke to him of the way of life. He treated her, he said, with scorn and rude contempt; she, however, meekly persisted in her work of mercy, and at length God rewarded her Christian zeal. He became a convert, and not a convert merely, but a confessor and sufferer for Christ. He had persecuted the little maid, but he had himself endured severer persecution since, having been imprisoned fourteen days on bread and water. We asked him if he did not feel it hard to be shut up in a dungeon, and treated as a criminal? His answer was worthy of a Christian. 'Not so hard,' he said, 'as to feel that I could not always trust in Christ.' Such men may be branded as fanatics, but assuredly it is the fanaticism of apostles and martyrs."*

During the stay of Dr. Steane and his colleague, the ordinance of baptism was administered on two occasions. On this subject Dr. S. writes as follows:

"Their baptisms have to be stealthily administered on some lone sea-shore, or in a hidden nook of some inland lake, where no hostile eye may see them, and no lurking policeman spring upon them. Some have been baptized since we have been here; but the blessed deed, as though it had been the perpetration of a great crime, was done at midnight,

* Notes of a Tour in Sweden, pp. 57-59.

and so secretly that even we heard nothing of it till afterward." On their asking why they were not informed of the baptism, as it would have given them pleasure to be present, Mr. Wiberg replied, "It is not necessary for *you* to break the law, although it is so for us. It is as well that you were not there."

He remarks further:

"There is a freshness and simplicity in the new religious life here, which contrasts strangely with the old fixed and conventional forms in which we are accustomed to see it. . . . The Baptists are acknowledged, even by their adversaries, to be a quiet, upright people, with whom no fault can be found but that they will be Baptists. The civil rulers would not persecute them; and some in authority assured me that the State clergy were the instigators of all the intolerant measures taken against them."

The members of the German deputation, Rev. J. G. Oncken, and J. Köbner, found a home with Mr. Wiberg during their visit, "where," writes Mr. Köbner, "brotherly love did every thing to make our stay agreeable."

They, as well as the English delegates, attended the meetings of the Evangelical Alliance. Mr. Köbner addressed the meeting in Danish, which language is intelligible to the Swedes. The others spoke in English, and Mr. Wiberg acted as their interpreter. Mr. Köbner says:

"Very important and interesting subjects were discussed. Sweden is the land where religious liberty is under the severest legal restraint, and yet I never heard such freedom of speech in any similar assembly. Even the Baptists occupied a very important position, and the opportunity to express their sentiments was as freely and as fully granted to them as to the ministers and other members of the State Church."

Of the impression left by their intercourse with the Baptists in Sweden, Mr. Köbner thus writes:

"I conceived a strong affection for the Swedish brethren, and esteem them highly—so full of heart and life, and so intelligent and prudent in expression. Heart and mind so sweetly blend in them, that one feels quite at ease in their conversation and debates."

The impression left on the minds of the English delegates is thus given:

"It was a most interesting assembly. Composed of young, energetic, well-informed and good-tempered men, men clear in their distinguishing views, both of dissent and baptism; men determined to labor for God, and ready to suffer—many of them had already suffered for Him; men who knew how to act, not only alone, but together, for not a trace of disorder appeared in their proceedings—it seemed to be the very nucleus of a living society, destined not only to perpetuity, but to augmentation. Certainly what we saw made us love them fervently, and we were strongly impressed with the conviction that, for the Baptists in Sweden, at least—to apply a saying of Dr. Krummacher, of Berlin—'there is a future.'"

At the close of the Conference it was resolved, in consideration of the time occupied, and the expense incurred in traveling, to hold the meetings hereafter triennially instead of annually.

During this summer, about forty persons were added by baptism to the church in Stockholm. Among these was Mr. Schyberg. This gentleman has built a large hall for worship in connection with his residence, in the south part of Stockholm. This is a considerable distance from the usual place of worship of the church, and meetings there are very numerously attended. Throughout this summer Mr. Wiberg preached there almost every Sunday evening. These meetings in Schyberg's Hall have been continued regularly since.

The Colporteurs' School, in connection with the Missionary Union of Stockholm, is continued during the six winter months, and has been very useful.

A Dorcas Society, which was formed in connection with the church in the winter of 1857, has been the means of doing much good.

CHAPTER VIII.

DALECARLIA.

A PECULIAR interest attaches itself to the province of Dalecarlia, or Dalarna, as it is often called. Here the heroic Gustavus Wasa, in the disguise of an humble peasant, sought a secure retreat after the massacre at Stockholm, in which his father and nearly one hundred of the principal nobles of Sweden were slain by command of the sanguinary Christian. In the Dalecarlian mines Gustavus labored for his daily bread, awaiting the time when he might rise and rescue his country from the yoke of the oppressor. Yet even this lowly occupation and humble disguise was insufficient for his concealment.

A woman with whom he lodged noticed the embroidery on the collars of his under garments, and soon it was whispered through the mine, and in the village, that their fellow-workman was a noble in disguise. The rumor reached the ears of Rankhitta, the lord of the mines. He at once visited the mines, and quickly recognized Gustavus, who had been his fellow-student at the University of Upsala. He generously invited him to his house.

DALECARLIAN PEASANTS.

Thither Gustavus repaired in secret, and many plans were talked over between him and his friend for the delivery of their country from the Danish oppressors. But Rankhitta was timid, and could not sympathize with the ardent courage and the eager pantings of freedom which animated the heart of Gustavus. He left him, and sought the residence of another noble, who received him with simulated friendship. But soon learning his treacherous designs, Gustavus left his house under cover of the night, and after many perils and escapes he found himself under the protection of a priest whose heart burned with patriotic zeal, and who was thoroughly acquainted with the character both of the nobles and of the peasants of these valleys and hills.

Following his host's advice, which his own observation fully confirmed, Gustavus resolved no longer to confer with the nobles, but to address himself at once to the warm and patriotic hearts of the peasantry. It is well known that a strong love of freedom and of their native land characterizes the inhabitants of mountainous countries. The highlanders of Scotland and mountaineers of Switzerland afford examples of this love of country, and the warm-hearted, hardy sons of Dalecarlia are well worthy to rank with the countrymen of Bruce and of Tell.

Annual festivals were held in the parish of Mora, at the head of Lake Siljan. And these festivals

10*

were attended by very large numbers of the peasantry.

Lake Siljan is situated nearly in the centre of Dalecarlia, and the aspect of the country on its borders is in striking contrast with the wild and mountainous districts by which it is surrounded. Well-cultivated fields and comfortable homesteads afford pleasing evidence of the industry of the inhabitants.

Here, in December, 1520, at the Christmas festival, Gustavas Wasa appeared before the assembled multitude. The earnest eloquence with which he dwelt on the wrongs which they had already endured, and the still greater miseries which were in store for them through Danish oppression, stirred every heart to resist the invader.

A curious circumstance is mentioned by a Swedish historian, indicative of the superstitions of the country. The old men in the assembly watched the wind, and observed that it had blown constantly from the north during the harangue of Gustavus. This was deemed among them as an infallible token of success. They felt assured of the Divine approbation, and a company of four hundred men placed themselves under the command of Gustavus.

Well-directed enterprises and successes which, though trifling in themselves, augured well for the future, soon caused the whole province to declare in favor of Gustavus, and in a short time he found himself at the head of 15,000 men.

Complete success at length crowned the efforts of the heroic Gustavus. The union of Calmar, which had been productive of such fatal results to Sweden, was broken, the Danish yoke was shaken off, and by general acclamation Gustavus Ericson Wasa, the descendant of their ancient kings, was placed upon the throne of Sweden. What important events were thus brought about, originating in the patriotic ardor and determined courage of the band of Dalecarlian peasants assembled on the shores of Lake Siljan!

The Dalecarlians of the present day appear to retain, in a great degree, the characteristics of their ancestors in the days of Gustavus Wasa. Travelers in Sweden speak with enthusiasm of the sturdy, handsome, warm-hearted Dalecarlian peasant. Love of his native country, and especially of Dalarna, burns as strongly in the heart of the Dalecarlian of our day, as it did in the hearts of his forefathers when, at the voice of Gustavus, they rose and struck the first blow in that struggle which freed Sweden from the yoke of the Dane.

The natural position of the country is favorable to this love of country and love of liberty. Dalecarlia, or the Dales, comprises chiefly the two great river basins and numerous side branches of the West and East Dal rivers, called in Swedish, Wester Dal and Oester Dal. These rivers take their rise in the mountainous regions in the north-western part of the province, where mountain, ravine, cataract, and pine forest, succeed each other in almost endless succession. From this wild and romantic region the two rivers descend into the more peaceful and fertile scenes in the country below. We have already mentioned the pleasing appearance of the fields and farms on the shores of Lake Siljan. It is below this lake that the two rivers unite and form the Dal.

The inhabitants of these valleys retain more of their ancient simplicity of manners, dress, and mode of living, than the natives of any other part of Sweden. This is owing, in part, to their isolated position, which has preserved them in a great degree from the vice and immorality which prevails to a fearful extent in other parts of Sweden, especially in Stockholm. And also in part to the fact of their esteeming themselves—as is often found to be the case among mountaineers—a superior race to their more lowland neighbors in the south. During the summer months, large numbers, both of men and women, especially from the more sterile districts, repair to Stockholm to obtain work. Their strength, industry, and proverbial honesty, cause them to be very generally employed in that city. Others again wander much further from home, and visit Russia, Italy, England, and other countries of Europe, to sell the products of their ingenuity and industry—basket-work, watches, hair-chains, bracelets, etc. But however far he may wander, or however lucrative the employment in which he may be engaged, the heart of the Darlecarlian still fondly turns toward home, and the approach of winter finds him once more among his native mountains and valleys, which the charms of no other country can ever rival in his eyes.

The influence which the parish priests exert over this true-hearted, simple-minded people, is very great. Their duties are by no means confined to the spiritual guidance and instruction of the people. They are the school-managers, the leaders of education, the chief representatives in the Diet, and the legal advisers of their flocks. They also possess the influence which wealth ordinarily gives. For their incomes from tithes, fees for baptisms, marriages, and funerals, and other offerings, amount to from $3000 to $4000 a year. This is a very large income in the interior of Sweden, and enables the parish priest to exercise an almost unlimited hospitality.

The following extracts from the journal of a traveler, who spent the summer of 1856 in Sweden and Norway, present a vivid picture of a Sunday among the Dalecarlians, and enable us to form some idea of the intercourse subsisting between pastor and people; and also of the kind of instruction which is likely to be imparted by such a pastor to his flock. It offers a strange spectacle to our eyes—the minister standing in the morning by the open grave, or distributing the bread and wine at the Lord's table, and in the evening drinking punch and whiskey, and watching with pleasure the gay whirl of the waltz.

The writer was staying at Leksand, at the southern extremity of Lake Siljan, in the parish of the Domprosten H., whose parsonage contains twelve thousand people, and has forty-six schools.

"LEKSAND, *August.*—The sight yesterday morning (Sunday) at the church was one of the most impressive I ever saw. I rose at half-past six, in a cool, brilliant summer morning, and the people were even then beginning to straggle into the great church-yard—the women arranging their *toilettes* in the angles of the church walls. At seven a fleet of boats from various parts of the lake were flashing and plowing through the water, all directed toward one point, and pulling with a regular strong beat, as in a boat race. At one time I counted thirty-one large boats, with thirty or forty people in each. They were all in costume, and the boats glistened with white and red, as if it were some festal procession. As each struck the land, it emptied itself of the brilliantly-dressed party—the women in broad, white head-dresses, and with red bodies; the men wearing long black coats, sometimes with embroidery on the shoulders, and black 'Kossuth hats.' As they came up the hill, with their various colors fresh in the morning sun, they formed a most picturesque train. Each

LAKE SILJAN, AND CHURCH OF LEKSAND.

one carried the psalm book, wrapped in a neat cloth, and those in the rear bore the baskets of biscuits and onions for the meal after service.

"The men were much the finer looking, though the women had hearty, pleasant, sun-brown faces, with very white teeth, while there were some young girls of exquisite and regular features.

"By eight o'clock the streets of the little village were crowded with a great multitude of peasants. From land and from water they came pouring into the church-yard. Soon a denser crowd gathered around a particular spot—a sad procession, with hearse and mourners, entered—the young *Comminister* read the service over the grave, and the whole multitude in the open air joined in a grand, solemn hymn. At the same time another large company were receiving the Communion in one part of the church.

"At half-past ten, when I entered, an imposing spectacle met the eye. The spacious church,—with its two tiers of galleries, its long seats and aisles, was crowded to the full; the chandeliers and little pronged supports were black with hats, and every available standing-place was filled—all by the peasants alone. I saw but one lady's bonnet and gentleman's coat in the house. It was a vast array of stalwart-looking men and ruddy, sun-burned women in their particolored picturesque costume. All were there—the nursing-child and the hobbling old man—no one was left at home. The men took the seats first; those who stood up in the aisles were women. Some of the mothers were feeding their infants with onions.

"As each person entered he stopped a moment, covered his face, and made a silent prayer. After a little time a hymn was commenced by the congregation—a monotonous, melancholy kind of chant. The organ was a powerful one, but it was almost drowned in the surges of sound which rolled up from that vast assembly. This was continued through some thirty or forty verses. At length the clergyman ascended the pulpit; a short, apparently extempore, prayer was uttered; and the sermon was read. There was profound attention through the whole audience. After it a quartette was sung with beautiful effect; and with another long chant, and some reading of the Scriptures, the assembly dispersed. Many lingered without to admire the new crown just placed on the Byzantine-like tower, others gathering in knots to discuss business and village affairs.

"My friends computed that there were seven thousand persons present in the church.

"I was impressed, in seeing the audience, with the wonderful opportunities granted to the Swedish clergy for influence over the peasants. In such remote provinces they are almost the sole guides and directors—there are no nobles, or judges, or governors here, and every Sunday they have these vast audiences upon which to impress humane, liberal and religious sentiments. The Swedes are plainly susceptible to oratory, and there never was such a field for a great Reformer as Sweden is now. But who is there will come forward to work it?

"We are occupying the lower rooms of the parsonage—large, pleasant rooms in one of the houses; above us are the saloons for company. On the other side of the square is the kitchen and servants' house; and on still another side, the house for the pastor's family. The doors are all open, and in the kitchen department is observed a number of the poor peasants taking food; in the pastor's saloon a little table is bounteously filled, from which we are to take and eat, wherever we can find a seat. A glass of whiskey, and bread and anchovies, are offered to each first, as usual. A number of persons come in and join us in the meal. The servants bring in course after course, in most liberal measure. After the dinner we start for a long walk by the pleasant lake, while the *Prost* goes to the parish meeting.

"Sunday evening at the pastor's is the *fête* evening, always; but more especially now, as they wish to celebrate the raising of the Church tower.

"The large guest saloons are thrown open, as well as the state bed-chamber, and by six o'clock the guests begin to come. The gentlemen are in one room and the ladies in another, and as each gentleman enters he shakes hands with the pastor, and then with every other gentleman; he then goes through the ladies' rooms, bowing to each very low and formally, seldom shaking hands. The ladies go through a similar ordeal—each one bowing and courtesying all through our saloon to every gentleman whom she knows."

The guests at this *levée* appear to have been chiefly *burgers*, with perhaps one or two nobles. Only three peasants, or Bonders, are mentioned as being present. One of these is the delegate to the parliament; the two others are the workmen who placed the crown finally on the tower, and who are the heroes of the evening.

After conversation of a desultory nature, punch in small glasses was brought. The pastor stepped forward and proposed several toasts in succession. After these were drunk, dancing began. "The great saloon shook with the tread of the dancers. The Comminister, who spoke at the grave and led the Communion in the morning, was now moving cheerily among the waltzers, though not dancing himself."

After the dance popular melodies were sung. At ten o'clock the company went across the square, where, in a large saloon, a table was spread. Meats, puddings, game, pancakes, milk-soup, salad, *gröt* (or rye-mush) and milk, fish, cakes, and creams, formed a very substantial repast. Nothing was drunk at the meal except the unfailing prelude of a glass of whiskey, until later, when the servants brought in a great silver flagon, with curious ornamenting, foaming with beer. This was a gift from a former parish to the pastor. It was passed around, each drinking in turn. At twelve the company began to disperse, the pastor giving good-night, with a shake of the hand, to each departing guest."

CHAPTER IX.

BAPTISTS IN DALECARLIA.

A RECENT traveler in Sweden, after speaking of the quiet, earnest way in which the Baptists in that country are laboring for the advancement of the great principles of Christianity, proceeds to say:

"They have thus far suffered persecution, banishment, and reproach, but each day their cause grows stronger, and takes deeper hold of the hearts of the people."

As we trace the progress of Baptist principles in Dalarna, we must remember all the obstacles which impede their onward course. All the wealth and power and influence of the hierarchy are employed to crush out this "heresy," and to silence the voice of the preacher. Blows, fines, and imprisonments, are meted out both to pastor and people. Men cast out their names as evil, and, often, friends and relatives disown them. Yet, notwithstanding all these trials and difficulties, we find in Dalarna, as in other parts of Sweden, the cause of God and of truth steadily advancing.

A copy of Mr. Wiberg's first work on Baptism, "Who is to be baptized?" was taken to Dalarna during the time that its author was in the United States. It was first read by Nas Per Person. He was convinced, by reading this work and carefully searching the Scriptures, that it was his duty to be baptized. He loaned the book to others. A powerful religious movement commenced about this time in Dalarna, and the little volume was eagerly read by many who were seeking to know and to do whatsoever the Lord commanded. It went from hand to hand until it was worn out. Many from its perusal were led to see their duty, and expressed an anxious desire to be baptized.

In May, 1854, P. F. Hejdenberg, who had himself been aroused to seek after the truth by the perusal of this book, went to Hamburg to visit the Baptist Church there and to request baptism. He was baptized by Rev. J. G. Oncken, and he was subsequently ordained. On his return Mr. Hejdenberg baptized the believers who were awaiting the ordinance, and they were organized into churches.

Three of these churches, containing an aggregate of about two hundred and seventy members, were organized in Dalarna, in the parishes of Orsa and Elfdahlen, and at Ona, in the parish of Mora. By reference to the statistics, it will be seen that these churches have been since steadily increasing in numbers. In the following year the church in Womhus was organized, and in 1857 another was formed in Bonas. This last-named church, as well as that of Ona, is in the parish of Mora.

During the summer of 1857, the preaching of the word was greatly blessed in this region, many were brought to trust in the Saviour, and were baptized in his name. Trials and persecutions of various kinds followed those who thus dared to obey God rather than man. They were summoned before tribunals, civil and ecclesiastical, fined, imprisoned on bread and water, and, often, the rites of marriage were denied to those Baptists who were unable to pay a fee sufficiently large to overcome the scruples of the priest. The Lutheran priests refused to perform the marriage ceremony for those who were not communicants in the State Church; and ministers of any other church are forbidden to perform this ceremony, under penalty of three years' imprisonment in a fortress, at hard labor. In order that their ministers might not incur this penalty, persons, in several instances, united themselves in presence of the assembled church, plighting their vows to each other in a solemn manner. An information was laid against a minister merely because, at the close of a meeting he had implored the blessing of God on those who had thus united themselves. And during this year, (1857) several, who were thus united, were fined and separated by the authorities in Dalarna.

Their minister shared in the sufferings of his flock; he was pursued with unrelenting animosity;

in one instance he was cruelly attacked, and beaten about the head, yet he relaxed not in his efforts. In the latter part of the summer, a fellow-laborer in the gospel visited Mora, and finding the pastor depressed from ill health added to many difficulties, he cheered him by reminding him of the state of things in Mora and Womhus three years before, when first he came there. The review of all that the Lord had wrought caused him to thank God and take courage. And with the prayer that "the Lord would give him more grace not to be overcome by the difficulties of the way," he determined to labor on faithfully.

Thus these fellow-laborers in the Lord's vineyard cheer and encourage each other. Partakers now of each others' labors, sharers in contumely, reproach, and suffering, they will be partakers in that glorious reward which the Lord, the righteous Judge, will bestow on His faithful ones in the last Great Day.

During this year the church at Mora commenced making efforts to build a house of worship. They secured a spot of ground, and commenced hewing and hauling timber on the ground. Their efforts were much impeded by the poverty of the members. But they persevered, and in the spring of 1859, when Mr. Wiberg made a tour in Dalarna, he preached in the new Baptist meeting-house to a congregation of about four hundred persons. It is a neat and comfortable frame building, entirely completed, with the exception of the gallery, which was not yet finished. At Elfdahlen, also, they have a convenient house of worship. The church, here numbers two hundred and sixty members. Here Mr. Wiberg preached during this tour, on a week-day, to a congregation numbering, both in the morning and the evening, about five hundred persons. Earnest attention and deep interest were manifested. A day or two afterward Mr. W. received a visit early in the morning from a church warden, who was very anxious on the subject of baptism. He was subsequently led to see clearly the path of duty, and was baptized in obedience to the Saviour's command.

The efforts of the Baptists to awaken a true interest in religion in the minds of the people, have roused the zeal and activity of the Lutherans in this region. Formerly no week-day religious meetings were ever heard of. But now they hold them frequently in almost every village. Sometimes every day in the week, and regularly on Wednesdays and Saturdays.

At Womhus, also, a house of worship is erected. Here Mr. Wiberg preached, and the congregation was so large that many went away, unable even to find a standing-place where they might hear. An associational meeting of the churches in Dalarna was held with the church at Womhus, while Mr. W. was with them.

During the tour of Mr. Wiberg, another Baptist

Church was organized in Dalarna. The history of its origin will be read with interest.

In the fall of 1857, one of the Colporteurs of the PUBLICATION SOCIETY, Nas Per Person, visited Norberg. He, as we have seen, was the first person in Dalarna who read Mr. Wiberg's book on Baptism. He was a native of Orsa. His mother is a pious woman and a member of the Baptist Church, and his sister, Anna Persdotter, has twice suffered imprisonment on bread and water for her adherence to Baptist principles. As early as 1853 Nas Per Person began to labor earnestly for the spread of the gospel in his native place, and in the neighboring parish of Mora. He was gladly listened to by the people; his gentle and winning manners gained their confidence, and often converted bitter opposers into warm friends. The priests strove to silence him, first by threats, and afterward by fines and imprisonment; but he continued to preach in the name of Jesus. His preaching was made the power of God unto salvation to many souls. A few years later,—in the autumn of 1856,—a check was put to his efforts for the spread of the gospel, by the refusal of the authorities in his native place to grant him a passport. He therefore determined to remove with his family to Böllnas, in the province of Helsingland. From this place he was able to travel as Colporteur into the neighboring parishes, and also into his native province of Dalarna.

In one of his tours, the following year, he visited Norberg, as before mentioned. There had never been any religious meetings held in this parish, except the usual religious services of the State Church. The people listened with surprise to the earnest, soul-stirring exhortations of the stranger who had come to speak to them of the Saviour. Accustomed to the cold, formal round of mere external religious observances, the stated and compulsory attendance at the Lord's Supper,—where the drunkard, the profane, and the worldly, were equally welcome with the humble, sincere Christian,—the doctrine, "Except a man be born again, he cannot enter the kingdom of God," sounded in their ears as a new and startling announcement.

A gentleman of influence in this neighborhood, Mr. Kjerrulf, the owner of extensive ironworks, took a deep interest in the progress of the good work. He conveyed the colporteur from one place to another in his own carriage, which caused this humble servant of God to exclaim, in a letter written about this time, "How wonderful! I who have been accustomed to be carried in a prisoner's car, to be thus honored! Praised be the Lord for all!" A few evenings later a meeting was held at the ironworks, and all the men were permitted to cease work that evening and attend the meeting.

In the spring of 1859, two gentlemen from Dalarna visited Stockholm. They came to converse with Mr. Wiberg, and to present themselves before the Church in Stockholm as candidates for baptism. They were received, and the following morning, at a very early hour, Mr. Wiberg went three miles out of the city to administer to them the ordinance. These gentlemen were Mr. K. and the foreman of his works, who had traveled one hundred and twenty miles to comply with the command of the Saviour.

The following month, at the close of a tour in Dalarna, Mr. Wiberg visited Presthyttan, Mr. Kjerrulf's residence. He was gladly welcomed. Mr. K. had built, adjoining his residence, a hall for religious meetings, capable of containing from two to three hundred persons. Here Mr. Wiberg preached for two or three evenings. There were a number of candidates for baptism who presented themselves the following Sunday morning, 22d of May. In the afternoon Mr. Wiberg preached. In the evening they repaired to a lake in the vicinity, where, in the presence of about two hundred spectators, Mr. Wiberg buried in baptism twenty-three rejoicing believers. The lake being on Mr. K.'s estate, they had nothing to fear from assailants. The scene was deeply impressive, and, as one present remarked, it was "a season that will tell on coming generations." On returning from the water they assembled in the meeting-room, and there organized the first Baptist Church at Presthyttan, consisting of thirty-seven members. The Lord's Supper was then celebrated, and the interesting services of this eventful day did not close till the night was far advanced. The following morning after an early prayer-meeting, Mr. Wiberg pursued his homeward journey. Mr. K. took him in his carriage to the town of Westeras, a good day's journey from Presthyttan. And thence, the following morning, he returned by steamboat to Stockholm.

By reference to the map, it will be seen that the organization of this church is an indication of the spread of Baptist principles in Dalarna. The religious movement in that province commenced in the parish of Orsa and its vicinity, and the five churches which were first constituted are all situated to the north of Lake Siljan, extending from that lake in a north-westerly direction. Norberg, near which Presthyttan is situated, is in the south-eastern extremity of the province.

CHAPTER X.

SKANIA.

SKANIA is a large and flourishing province in the southern extremity of Sweden. It comprises the two modern divisions of Christianstad and Malmö. It is a flat and fertile region, and this, added to good cultivation of the soil, renders Skänia one of the most productive parts of Sweden. Her farmers are rapidly increasing in wealth. Some Scotch farmers have settled here, and have endeavored, with a good degree of success, to introduce into this province improved methods of farming.

Halland, where Nilsson labored and suffered, and where the first Baptist church in Sweden was formed, adjoins this province, yet it was not till the year 1856 that the subject of believers' baptism began to be considered in Skänia. A great religious movement was going on; the colporteurs of the Missionary Union of Stockholm were preaching the word with earnestness and faithfulness; men were turning to the scriptures, which had been too much neglected, as their sole guide in faith and practice. It is not surprising that when the subject of believers' baptism was presented to their minds, coming, as it does, with all the weight of scripture practice and of scripture teaching to enforce it, men should have anxiously desired to obey their Lord's command. A number of Christians, among whom were several of the colporteurs, were anxious that Mr. Wiberg should come down to baptize them. It was not possible for him to leave Stockholm at that time. One of the preachers, an interesting young man by the name of Sven Svenson, felt it his imperative duty to be baptized immediately, and he came up to Stockholm for that purpose, intending to return as soon as possible. Mr. Wiberg baptized him on the 26th of October, and, by his advice, Mr. Svenson then entered the newly-formed colporteur school. Having excellent natural abilities, six months' training in this school enabled him to return to his field of labor better qualified to work thoroughly and successfully. He is a faithful, earnest laborer, and the grace of God has signally crowned his efforts. He has labored as a Colporteur of the "PUBLICATION SOCIETY."

The following account of his unwearied labors and severe persecution, on his first return to Skänia, will be read with deep interest.

"ULLSTORP, Jan. 1858.

"In the month of April, 1857, I left Stockholm and traveled to the south of Sweden, where I was born. Here I commenced, as I had done several years past, traveling around and preaching the word of God to the people. On my arrival here from Stockholm, there was not to be found in the entire region a single baptized believer excepting myself, but many had their minds made up on the subject. Very soon after I came home, a meeting was held of Christians who had embraced Baptist views, at which meeting I was present. It was a happy and joyful occasion to many. I baptized on that day two colporteurs, Hanner and Lindegren, and I received an urgent request to go to a place called Yngsjo, for the purpose of baptizing some Christians. When I came, there were more ready to receive baptism than I had imagined. After being satisfied with their Christian experience and religious views, I baptized fifty-nine. From there I traveled to a village called Henesta. Here forty-four received baptism, and the day following twenty-one. I there preached before an immense concourse of people, who assembled for several days in succession to hear the Word of God. A church was organized here of sixty-five members, and a brother by name of Jöns Anderson, a farmer, was ordained to take the oversight of them in the Lord. From here I traveled to a village named Grödby, a distance of thirty miles, where I baptized thirty-four. I remained here to preach the Word for several days, and a church was organized—Brother Nils Svenson was ordained to take the charge of them. From here I went to a village named Ullstorp, where a church of fifty-seven members was organized, which has since increased to one hundred.

"I now went back to Yngsjo, for the purpose of strengthening the newly-baptized believers. While there the following circumstances occurred. I was sitting quietly, one morning, explaining the word of God to some friends, when suddenly the house was filled with enemies of God and all righteousness. They pushed me off the chair on which I sat, giving me repeated blows on the head, and pulled out my hair by the roots. They then dragged me out of the house to another place, where they recommenced striking and kicking me."

At length they desisted, and the meekness with which the minister of Christ endured all their cruel and brutal treatment, endeavoring at intervals to speak to them from the word of God, seemed to touch the hearts of some of his persecutors. But the others urged them on, bringing them brandy in order more to inflame their passions. This succeeded, and they now took him to the district-sergeant, who had him placed in the county prison.

"It was noised abroad that I was in the prison, and the yard was soon filled with people who came to see the infamous 'baptizer.' And so clamorous was the mob to see me that the sergeant, to gratify them, had me brought out before them, when I was made the butt of their scoffs, jeers, and ridicule.

Some swore, and cursed me, while others laughed at me. One old gentleman spit in my face, and said that I ought to be destroyed. They had determined at first that I should remain in the county prison over night. But after I was shut in, so great was my joy that I had been counted worthy to suffer reproach for the cause of my Master, that I could not refrain from singing songs of praise and speaking the word of God to others within the prison. When they heard this, they begged the district-sergeant to have me sent to the provincial penitentiary that same evening. They arrived there with me about midnight. Here I was met by the jail-keeper with curses. They then proceeded to clip my hair close to my head, strip me of my clothes, and drench me with cold water; after which they put on me a prisoner's dress, of very coarse, thin, gray material, and threw me into a dark cell. As the weather was quite cold I was seized with a violent chill. But the Lord strengthened me, and so manifested himself to me that I was enabled to rejoice in Him, and to feel that I was not left alone. From this place I was removed to a cell where I could see. Here I remained three days, after which I was placed on a prisoner's car and driven to my native place in order to be set at liberty. So terribly had the people been frightened that even Christians were afraid to receive me into their houses. In every village, watch was set to arrest me in case I should cross the boundaries of the parish in which I lived.

"This state of things looked very dark and mysterious to me and to my friends. But when the prayers of the poor and the oppressed ascended from earth to heaven, the Lord heard and sent help. In His great goodness it was so ordered that I was able to borrow some money, with which I secured the use of a house about three miles from Ullstorp. This place I had fitted up to hold meetings in. In this house I now preach the word of life to large congregations every Sunday. There are now in this region eleven Baptist churches organized, where there was not a single Baptist to be be found in April, 1857. In this house of which I have spoken, we now hold quarterly meetings, at which all the churches are represented. The number of baptized Christians in this region is five hundred and thirty-five. Unity and love are prevailing, and it seems as if the Lord would do yet greater things among us. The enemies of the truth, however, still rage terribly against us. For fear of them, when we go out to preach, we are often obliged to lie concealed during the day and hold our meetings at the midnight hour. Several times they have been out pursuing me with loaded guns, in order to put an end to me. But the Lord has wonderfully preserved my life. It is very difficult for me to go out to preach abroad the word of God, because I fear I should not be long permitted to have my liberty; and if I am arrested for the third time, I should be made a prisoner at hard labor for several months."

Thus in the midst of persecutions, the Lord sustained and strengthened his servant, and these afflictions only increased his desire to spend and be spent for Christ.

In July, in this year, Mr. Wiberg visited Skänia, and spent two or three weeks in visiting different parts of that region. In reviewing his journeys during that summer, he writes:

"I am filled with gratitude to the Lord for what He has already done, and with most sanguine expectations for the future. Our churches here are but in their infancy, and need much watch, care and instruction, as they have but just emerged from the semi-papal darkness and superstition of the State Church. They have also to struggle with great difficulties, being poor, and persecuted, and some of the members living many miles apart. In several places they are destitute of able pastors and preachers, who might feed them with the bread of life. Especially is this the case in some parts of Skänia. There is, for instance, one church very far in the south and remote from the others, called Yngsjo,* which consists of seventy members. This

* The place where Mr. Svenson baptized the first band of believers, on his return from Stockholm, and where he was afterwards arrested and maltreated.

church has as yet neither pastor nor preacher, and they have not the means of sustaining one, being mostly fishermen and very poor. So great is the hostility against this little flock, that my friends solemnly warned me from going there, as the enraged mob might kill me. While I was at Christianstad, however, many of these brethren came to see me, and I endeavored to instruct and comfort them from the word of God. Brother Svenson has once or twice ventured to visit them, but he has been obliged to wend his way as through an encampment of enemies on the battle-field. Brother Segerstrom, from Mala, on a journey from Stockholm, ventured to stop one evening among them, but he was most shamefully maltreated, and barely escaped with his life from the infuriated mob. And, generally, our colporteurs can scarcely go without the borders of their respective parishes without being seized and imprisoned. On account of these persecutions, a few have returned to the State Church. Yet the cause of Christ is steadily and gloriously advancing through the whole of this southern region."

Several circumstances of peculiar interest occurred during this tour of Mr. Wiberg. We will therefore subjoin some extracts from his journal. He went first to Westervik, where he designed to take the steamer to Christianstad. He delayed doing so for a few days that he might visit the parish of Gamleby, twelve miles distant, the home of Mr. Rolander, who had been spending the previous winter as a student in the colporteur school, in Stockholm. Mr. W. writes: "In this place there is much spiritual darkness. About nine years ago only a solitary female was known here as a true, living Christian. Through her instrumentality Bro. Rolander was led to think of the concerns of his soul, and, as I trust, truly converted. This young brother has for some time been holding meetings in his father's house, and an interest seems to be awakened in the minds of some. He has long felt it his duty to be baptized, but deferred from a great desire to be baptized in his own native village.

"Saturday, 11th. Being fully satisfied of the genuineness of Bro. Rolander's piety and his views of gospel truth, we proceeded, at the close of the day, to a retired spot selected by Bro. R. himself, and there it was my privilege to baptize him in the likeness of his Saviour's death and resurrection. For fear of disturbance no spectator was allowed to be present. Both before and after baptism we knelt together in prayer on the sea-shore. It was a highly interesting season to us both.

"Sunday, 12th. Attended service in the State Church, which is only a few steps from Bro. R.'s house: his father is the organist. The priest read a sermon and christened four infants, whom he pronounced thereby born again and made inheritors of the kingdom of God. In the afternoon we had meeting at Bro. R.'s house, which was densely crowded. Being unwell myself, Bro. R. spoke with great power and clearness, and I followed with some concluding remarks. Many were affected to tears, and several remained for religious conversation."

Early the following morning the priest appeared at the house of Mr. Rolander, saying that he had been informed that the travelers who were staying were Baptists, and that he was come to call his son to an account for having introduced them into the parish. He was very angry, but hearing that they were going to leave immediately, he became pacified and left the house. Mr. R. accompanied him to Westervik, and was there ordained on the following day.

On the 16th, Mr. W. reached Christianstad. He writes:

"We were kindly received by a Christian friend, Mr. Hallberg. Although not a Baptist himself, he has done much to aid our cause. He has for a long time opened his house for religious worship, and during the last summer he has built an addition in the form of a meeting room capable of containing from three to four hundred persons. Yet his means are limited; he is a carpenter by trade. We had very interesting meetings here."

On Sunday, 19th, at four in the afternoon, about four hundred persons assembled for public worship. Mr. Wiberg preached. At nine in the evening the baptized believers in Christianstad assembled for the purpose of being organized into a regular Baptist Church. Mr. Struve was ordained as their pastor. After which they celebrated the Lord's Supper, and continued together in prayer until midnight.

"20th, at Bjernhult," writes Mr. W., "I was most heartily welcomed by a Christian sister, who has a very large house which she opened for worship. We commenced meeting at four o'clock; about five hundred persons were present. We continued together until ten o'clock in the evening. Bro. Nymanson,* a Colporteur, and myself, spoke. Much feeling was manifested. It was truly delightful to see so many of the young in the morning of life walking in the ways of the Lord. After the meeting I distributed about one thousand pages of tracts. We have here a church of seventy members, raised mainly through the instrumentality of Bro. Sven Svenson. After the close of the first meeting we held a special meeting of the church, at which I endeavored to impart to them such counsel and instruction as I thought would prove useful."

At Vinslof, where Mr. W. arrived on the 22d, he called on Dr. Bergman, a minister of the State Church, who received him very kindly, though he seemed distressed at the great increase of the Bap-

* He was one of the first to embrace Baptist views in Skänia, but worn out by persecutions, and impoverished by fines, he has since returned to the State Church.

tists in his vicinity. He invited Mr. W. to remain with him over night. And three of the Colporteurs, with whom Mr. W. had an appointment, having sought for him at the parsonage, were invited in, and thus there was opportunity for free discussion of Baptist doctrines and practices.

Happy would it be for Sweden if such instances of kindness and liberality of feeling were more numerous among the clergy of the State Church! Let us hope and pray for the spread of vital Christianity throughout the State Church: then persecution and oppression will cease, and every Christian will rejoice to meet in every other Christian a brother.

The following day, at Mala, Mr. W. met with Rev. S. Svenson, and other preachers. A meeting for worship was held, after which Messrs. Hanner and Segerstrom were ordained to the work of the gospel ministry. The latter has the pastoral charge of the little church in Mala, consisting then of twenty-seven members, which, before the close of 1858, had increased to one hundred.

"Saturday, 25th, I started early in the morning for Bjorkerod, a distance of twenty-four miles. Here I was gladly received by a distinguished personage of the nobility, by the name of Carl Gustaf Rutger Skytte, a lineal descendant of the great Gustavus Adolphus. This brother, with eight members of his family, has been baptized since the month of April. I have seldom seen a more joyful, orderly, and consistent family of Christians. Adjacent to his house he has erected a little chapel where our poor persecuted brethren come for shelter and worship. Bro. Skytte and his family have been themselves very much persecuted. The priest on one occasion met his wife a short distance from her house. After conversing with her for some time, he became so angry that he seized her violently by the arm and shook her, saying, "If it were not for the influence which they exerted, and the protection they offered to the poor people who flocked to them, he would very soon suppress the baptistical heresy prevailing in his parish."

Here Mr. W. preached on Sunday afternoon to a congregation of three hundred persons. In the evening a prayer and conference meeting was held.

"Monday, 27th. After morning prayer meeting I visited Bro. Lindegren, in Tagaröd, where there is a church of seventy members, including those who meet in the chapel of Bro. Skytte. Brother Lindegren exercises the pastoral care over the people. They have commenced building a house for him, which is to have a room added to it sufficiently large for a meeting room.

"In the evening I preached at Svenstorp, about three miles distant, before a very large and attentive congregation. I have seldom attended a more solemn meeting. I here met with Nils Hokanson, the blind Colporteur, who had been imprisoned at

Christianstad, and had been fettered with a chain on his ankle, for holding conventicles.

"Tuesday, 28th. Started for Paradis, a distance of thirty miles, and arrived there at six o'clock, P. M. When we were near to the place, we passed the district sergeant, who was on the alert for us, being apprized of our coming. He did not, however, for reasons unknown, follow us. When we arrived the house was already so crowded, that it was with difficulty we could press in. At the close of the meeting it was discovered that a mob had collected, who were armed with scythes, sickles, and stones, in order to attack persons on their way home. Most of our friends had to remain until morning."

The following morning Mr. W. went to Solvitzborg where he took the steamer for Carlshamn. Bro. Ramgren has charge of the little Baptist Church in this place. He told Mr. W. that the priest preached against the Baptists every Sunday, and so inflamed the minds of the people against them that he could not walk the streets without being insulted.

During the year 1858 persecution continued unabated. Sven Svenson ventured to leave Ullstorp in order to make a missionary tour, but he was soon arrested, thrown into chains, and taken back to his native parish.

From the last reports from this region it appears as if the violence of persecution had in some degree slackened. Sven Svenson preached in various places during the months of September, October, and November, without hindrance from the authorities. At Yngsjo he preached four times. At Carlshamn, though he was refused the hall, a Lutheran opened his house for worship, and he preached there in the evening. In some places riotous men endeavored by noise and by threats to disturb the meetings. But the priests do not appear to have interfered, except indeed so far as that their preaching and their hostility stir up the passions of the lowest order of the rabble.

During this tour Mr. Svenson had the joy of hearing from the lips of his father, who for several years had been an attentive hearer of the gospel, the cheering tidings that he had at length found peace in believing on the Lord Jesus Christ.

CHAPTER XI.

ISLAND OF GOTTLAND.

THE spread of Baptist principles has not been confined to the main land of Sweden. The Island of Gottland has been visited by our Colporteurs, and the preaching of these earnest and self-denying men has been crowned by the blessing of God.

This island is situated in the Baltic Sea, about seventy miles distant from the main land. It is about eighty miles in length, and thirty-three in breadth at the widest part. The climate is described as remarkably mild. Although it is in the same latitude as Labrador, the people do not reckon upon having more than eight days' sleighing in winter. Vegetables can be raised here, which will not grow on the main land of Sweden, and in favorable seasons and situations the walnut, the mulberry, and the grape, will ripen in the open air.

Wisby, the metropolis of the island, possesses much interest for the historian and the antiquarian. The period of its foundation is unknown; but in the tenth and eleventh centuries Wisby was one of the most important commercial cities in

Europe. While England was under Saxon domination, or torn by the fierce struggle between the Saxons and their Norman invaders, Wisby was a peaceful, wealthy, and flourishing city, the great emporium of the commerce of the north of Europe. The productions of the East were brought by caravans to Novogorod, in Russia, and thence across the Baltic to Wisby, where they met the furs, the copper, and the iron of Scandinavia. The towns of Italy had not yet risen to that commercial importance which they attained after the period of the Crusades, and the merchants from southern countries flocked to this northern market. Wisby rose in wealth and in importance. The architectural beauty displayed in the ruins of twelve churches, which date back to this period, affords interesting evidence of the magnificence of the city in those days; and the ancient wall, with its forty-five towers, encloses an area which might have sufficed for the habitation of thirty thousand or forty thousand people.

But the glory of Wisby has departed, and some four thousand five hundred inhabitants, dwelling for the most part in humble tenements, now occupy the places of its merchant princes, and scantily people its once busy, bustling streets.

The decline of Wisby dates from 1361, when it was stormed and sacked by Waldemar III., of Denmark. The plunder he obtained was enormous, as the city was the grand depot for all the merchandize of the Baltic. This was a fatal blow to the prosperity of the place.

Wisby is the only town of importance in Gottland. The population of the island, amounting to about forty-seven thousand inhabitants, is chiefly scattered in small villages, or on farms.

Throughout the whole island great spiritual darkness prevailed. The outward forms of worship, the ceremonials of the church, were carefully observed; but religion seemed to rest here. In the striking language of a Scotch gentleman, who visited Sweden in 1838:

"The clergy, and the people, appear to me to view Christianity altogether in a different light from that in which we view it. It is a different species of religion here."*

Within a few years past, however, the people have been rousing from this spiritual lethargy; and now, wherever the word of God is preached with faithfulness and earnestness, the people crowd to listen. Many conversions have taken place. There is opposition and persecution; but the good seed is sown, and is bringing forth fruit.

In the month of August, 1857, Mr. Wiberg visited this island. We find in one of his Diaries the following entry:

"August 2d, 1857. Arrived at the town of Wisby, in Gottland, at 6, A. M. Here the minds

* Laing's Tour in Sweden, p. 248.

of the people seemed to be awakened on the subject of religion; but there are no Baptists in the island. A Mr. Rechnitzer, a converted Jew, kindly allowed me to hold meeting in his house. I spoke from Matt. ii., before a goodly number."

The following morning Mr. Wiberg left the island, and returned to Stockholm.

Mr. Axel S. Rechnitzer, to whom reference is made in the foregoing extract, had for several years been preaching the gospel in different parts of the island, with much success. His thoughts were now turned to the question of believers' baptism. He made it a subject of earnest and prayerful consideration; and, as the result, we find him visiting Stockholm in the spring of 1858, for the purpose of receiving baptism. The ordinance was administered to him by Rev. A. Wiberg, in the night of May 27th. Mr. Rechnitzer returned to Gottland, and with earnestness and zeal continued his labors. His faithful efforts during the preceding years had prepared the field, and now, when he came among them with the exhortation, "Repent, and be baptized every one of you in the name of Jesus Christ," many were ready to respond to the call. Before the close of the year 1859, we find six Baptist Churches organized in Gottland, with an aggregate of three hundred and seventy-three members. The church in Wisby numbered thirty-two; the church in Hafdhem, on the western coast of the island, numbered one hundred and thirty-two, and the church in Hamra, in the southern part, numbered one hundred and eleven.

An instance of the earnest desire to spread the gospel in those who have been converted will be read with interest. An old man, eighty-two years of age, who for four years had been confined to his bed, felt an irresistible conviction that it was his duty to be baptized. His friends endeavored to dissuade him. Their remonstrances were unavailing; he was baptized. Soon afterwards he felt stronger and became able to walk about, his strength increasing every day. He resolved to use the remainder of his days and of his strength in going about among his old friends, to tell them what the Lord had done for his soul. He had been for many years a Representative of the island, and had a large circle of friends, among whom his words and exhortations had much weight. If this aged disciple thus labors in the evening of his days, what may not be expected from those who in life's prime, or in its early morning, are devoting themselves to the service of their Redeemer?

The good work, however, was not permitted to go on without opposition. The spirit of persecution was at once aroused. The new Conventicle Act was made use of by the priests, and the enforcement of its penalties was threatened against Mr. Rechnitzer, if he continued to act in the capacity of teacher. For a time he was obliged to desist from preaching or administering the ordinances; his place was filled by other brethren until they, in their turn, were prohibited. Mr. Rechnitzer was then summoned before the High Court of Stockholm, to answer various charges brought against him for preaching, baptizing, and administering the Lord's Supper. He appeared several times before the Court, to answer the numerous accusations which had been brought against him. His trial was postponed fourteen days in order to give him time to prepare his answer in writing, as the accusation filled from fifteen to twenty sheets of paper. At an interview which he had with the Councillor of Justice, he requested to have his case deferred to the next Diet, to which no objections were raised. However, he had to appear again, twice, before the Court, and answer questions on the views which he, and Baptists in general, held with regard to Baptism. On his last appearance, May 6th, his case was indefinitely postponed, and he was able to return to his post at Wisby. He had been detained, altogether, six weeks at Stockholm, and during this period he preached several times for the Baptist church in that city.

On his return to Wisby Mr. Rechnitzer visited the bishop, who received him in a very friendly manner, and, on his taking leave, requested him to repeat his visit, saying that it had been to him exceedingly interesting. A few days later, the bishop sent to desire to see him again, and, after a conversation of three hours, renewed his assurances of friendly feeling, and said that he would not hinder the meetings of the Baptists, provided they were not held at the hours of service of the State Church. He also publicly advised the priests to be tolerant towards the Baptists. That his injunctions have been obeyed, at least in Wisby, we gather from the following remarks:

"Nov., 1859. In Wisby, where persecution formerly was very severe, all persecution has now ceased, and we are permitted to assemble undisturbed, for devotional exercises, in various houses and rooms, which are crowded with people."

In a preaching tour which two of the colporteur preachers made, late in the fall of 1859, they preached in seventeen or eighteen different parishes, and in almost every case to large and attentive congregations. They were unmolested by the authorities during this tour, and in one parish—Grotlingbo—where Mr. Rechnitzer had been forbidden to preach under penalty of a fine of five hundred rix-dollars, neither priest nor church-council came to disturb the meeting. During this tour one Sunday-school and two churches were organized, and an associational meeting of the Baptist churches in Gottland was held at Gimringo: it was very numerously attended.

This relief from open and direct persecution by the authorities is a pleasing change, but by a reference to chapter fourteen, it will be seen that hostility assumes many forms, and perhaps the most painful of these are the great, almost insuperable, obstacles thrown in the way of the marriage of Baptists. They are also left wholly unprotected from attacks from any who choose to gratify their evil passions in that way. They have frequently to go several miles in order to administer the ordinance of baptism. The following will serve as an instance:

"October 2d, 1859. We went three miles out from Wisby for the purpose of administering the ordinance of baptism. We encountered many difficulties from the boatmen and people on the seashore. At last we retreated under a mountain, which rose two hundred feet above the level of the sea, and under its shelter we performed the solemn rite. Then the people went up to the summit of the mountain. They could not see us, but they could hear us; and, to gratify their malignant feelings, they threw down a quantity of gravel to annoy us."

The number of visitors who come to the house of the pastor of the church in Wisby, shows that an earnest spirit of inquiry is abroad among the people. One day he records: "I received the visits of twenty persons with whom I conversed on the subject of religion." A day or two later: "I conversed with ten inquirers, one of whom desired baptism." Scarcely a day passes but some persons present themselves at his house, seeking conversation and instruction. Sometimes those appear whom he had little expected. For instance, one day the sister of a Lutheran priest came to seek counsel of him. She and her husband had been among the bitterest opposers of the Baptists, but now she came with a penitent and humbled heart, and shed tears of mingled sorrow and joy.

This is not an isolated case. Many of the most violent opposers of the Baptists have, in different places, experienced the power of God's converting grace, and are now enrolled in the ranks of those whom formerly they despised and persecuted.

In Sundre, about eight miles from Hamra, and the most southern parish in Gottland, Mr. Rechnitzer preached in the house of one who, on a former occasion, had lain in wait to beat him, so great was his hatred to the Baptists! But the grace of God had touched his heart; he had been himself baptized, and now he rejoiced to receive into his house the servants of Christ. After holding an interesting meeting in his house, Mr. R. remarked:

"There is a vast difference now in the feelings of the people from what they were on my first visit four years ago, when at the hazard of my life I preached the gospel in this parish."

There is a regiment stationed in the island of Gottland, which, from its position in the Baltic, is a very important out-post of the Swedish dominions. Among this company of soldiers are to be found those who are ready to "endure hardness as good soldiers of Jesus Christ." In one of the prayer meetings of the church at Wisby, we find four officers and six corporals present, and engaging in prayer with the people of God. Six of these Christians, during the time their regiment was stationed at Wisby, lodged at the house of Mr. Rechnitzer, who speaks with joy of their fervent zeal. The memoirs of General Havelock and Captain Vicars, show that it is no easy work to hold fast a Christian profession in the army, where temptations are on every hand, and scoffers abound. But their bright examples show also that, though not easy, it is possible to attain to an eminent degree of piety, even in the camp, when the grace of God is in the heart. We rejoice in reading of these instances of His mercy in the Swedish army.

In the words of Mr. Rechnitzer, in reviewing the past, "we have special cause to take courage, and raise our voices in thanksgiving for what God has done for us."

CHAPTER XII.

WESTER NORRLAND AND ALAND.

SUNDSVALL, in the province of Medelpad, is prettily situated at the head of a bay, and is surrounded by steep hills. Its sheltered situation favors the growth of a variety of trees, which add much to the beauty of the place, and contrast agreeably with the vast fir forests of the surrounding region. The town contains about three thousand inhabitants, and derives much importance from its position, at the point of junction of the high roads to Trondhjem, in Norway, and Tornea, on the frontier of Russian Lapland.

This town, and its vicinity, was the scene of the unwearied labors of Rev. P. F. Hejdenberg, during the years 1855 and 1856, and in this place he has now fixed his residence. In August, 1855, Mr. Hejdenberg was summoned to appear before the Court of Orsa, in Dalarna, to answer the charges of holding conventicles and of departing from the church. He was in Stockholm at the time, and he determined to go to Orsa by the way of Norrland, hoping that while on his way he might have an opportunity of promoting the kingdom of Christ in that region. He arrived in Sundsvall, August 12th, and remained there ten days. During that time he held one or two meetings daily, generally in the open air. From four hundred to five hundred persons attended these meetings; sometimes their number increased to one thousand. The people listened with great eagerness, and the word seemed to affect their hearts.

He left Sundsvall for Orsa, August 22d; here he appeared before the Court, and also held meetings nearly every day. Nas Per Person was at this time preaching in Dalarna, and baptized ten persons in Lake Siljan, the day after Hejdenberg's arrival in Orsa. His answer before the Court having been made, he returned to Sundsvall, occupying three weeks on the journey, and preaching almost every day to congregations of three hundred or four hundred persons.

He reached Sundsvall, September 22d, having been absent a month. The seed which had been sown during his visit, in August, was now bringing forth fruit. A deep religious feeling prevailed, and many appeared to be truly converted. He remained nearly three weeks among them, during which time sixty-nine believers were baptized; some in Sundsvall, the others in the surrounding parishes.

On his return to Stockholm, he received a summons to appear before the Court of Skullersta, in Nerike, to answer a charge of having held conventicles. He obeyed the summons, holding, on his way thither, several meetings. Scarcely had he returned to Stockholm—the week following Mr. Wiberg's arrival from America—when he received another summons to appear before the Court in Sundsvall, on similar charges. He arrived in that place November 14th, and preached the word of God to large congregations, until the 26th, the day appointed for his appearance before the Court. His case was postponed to December 31st. He spent the interval in preaching in four of the neighboring parishes, where great anxiety was manifested to hear the word. At the close of the month he went to Sundsvall for the completion of his trial, and preached there during the week of his stay.

A summons from the Court of Orsa obliged Mr. Hejdenberg to leave Sundsvall for Dalarna, on January 5th, 1856. During this journey, he spent a month preaching almost daily to large congregations in Dalarna, and on his way to and from Orsa. Another summons from the Court of Sundsvall brought him back to that place, Febuary 24th, and here he remained till March 12th, having many opportunities to preach the gospel to the people.

During this last visit to Sundsvall, and its vicinity, forty-seven believers were baptized by Mr. Hejdenberg and Mr. Engberg, making, together with those baptized on his previous visit, one hundred and sixteen believers in the town of Sundsvall, and the adjoining parishes.

The church, in Sundsvall, suffered a great loss in the year 1858, in the removal, by death, of their pastor, Rev. Johan Engberg. He was among the first who were baptized in Sundsvall, by Mr. Hejdenberg. He was ordained to the work of the ministry, and settled as pastor of the Baptist Church in that place. The church, at the time of his death, numbered about one hundred and sixty members. Mr. Wiberg writes of him, as follows :

"He was a very devoted, self-sacrificing Christian. For several years past he opened his house for religious meetings, and from the organization of the church until the time of his death, the whole of his house, consisting of five rooms on the first floor, was opened every Lord's day, and almost every night in the week, for worship and other religious meetings. His labors were very much blessed, both in the town and in the country districts around Sundsvall. The interests of his church, until his last moments, lay heavily upon his heart, and his dying prayer was, that they might continue faithful, and stand forth as a beacon light before the world. He died September 6th, 1858, aged forty-nine years. Rev. P. F. Hejdenberg, for the present, fills the place made vacant by his death."

This church occupies a very important position, for in the surrounding parishes there are thirteen small Baptist Churches, numbering from twenty to eighty members, which stand connected with the church in Sundsvall, and many of the members of these churches attend the meetings at Sundsvall.

In August and September, 1856, Rev. Nas Per Person made a tour in the southern part of Helsingland, visiting Gefle, Soderhamn, Mo, Regnsjo, Bollnas, and other places. The people received him gladly, but the opposition of the priests was very great. At Soderhamn the interference of the town-sergeant prevented any meeting from being held. At Arbro the priest himself ordered Nas Per Person away. He had attended the meeting, and he said he found no fault with the discourse, but he feared if the colporteur remained he might propagate error. Notwithstanding opposition many believed the word and turned to God, especially in the parishes of Mo and Regnsjo.

In this last place a small church was constituted in the following year. In Mr. Wiberg's diary we find a short account of its pastor, Rev. Per Person:

"July 4th, 1857. I received a visit from a farmer living in Regnsjo, Helsingland, by the name of Per Person, with whom I had a long and interesting conversation. He expressed a desire to receive baptism, having been brought to a conviction of the truth by reading my book on that subject. He is a man of a literary cast of mind; he has a library of his own, and reads much. As a Christian he is devoted and zealous, and does much to keep up the religious interest in his parish."

Two days after Per Person, was baptized and ordained to the work of the ministry, and still continues in charge of the church in Regnsjo.

In the Island of Aland (Russia), situated in the Baltic, there has been gathered a little band of baptized believers. In the fall of 1854, Mr. Möllersvärd and another Baptist was sent by Mr. Forssell on business to the island of Aland. When the business was finished Mr. Möllersvärd remained to preach the Gospel. Hundreds attended the meetings which he held, and great interest was manifested. In the spring of 1856, an Alander came to Stockholm for the purpose of receiving baptism. Soon after his return he was summoned to appear before the priests. He underwent an examination of four hours before the arch-deacon. The district-sergeant searched his house for books, but they found none. He was then threatened with banishment, but no farther proceedings were instituted against him. Notwithstanding all this he ventured to hold meetings in his house, at which about fifty persons attended.

In November of the same year, two other Alanders visited the church in Stockholm for the purpose of receiving baptism. After giving satisfactory evidence to the church, they were received and baptized. And as a letter from Aland expressed the strong desire of a number of persons in the island that one of these brethren should be ordained to the Gospel ministry, Mr. Fagerström received ordination, and after remaining some days in Stockholm, they both returned home, followed by the prayers of the church.

In the following month the first baptism was administered in Aland. Soon after Mr. F. was summoned to appear before a civil tribunal to answer to a charge of apostasy. On that very day, soon after the district-sergeant had left, two persons came to request baptism, one of whom had been heretofore a bitter opposer, but was now an humble penitent. They have formed themselves into a church of eight members. May this little band exert a pure and Christian influence over multitudes around them, and many be added to them of such as shall be saved!

CHAPTER XIII.

SWEDISH LAPLAND.

The Society's colporteurs, in pursuing their unwearied labors for the salvation of men, have reached the most northern parts of Sweden, and preached the life-giving word in the barren regions of Swedish Lapland. The inhabitants of the province of Umea, or West Bothnia, are principally of Swedish, Finnish, and some of German origin, especially near the coast. In the interior are found the Laplanders, or Lapps. They are a wandering people, moving from place to place with their tents and herds of reindeer. They have some small villages, numbering from one hundred to two hundred inhabitants. But, in general, they lead a nomadic life. Their number amounts to about four thousand. It is among this people that the earnest and devoted Lœstadius spent his life. He died in 1841, but the deep religious feeling awakened by his preaching died not with him. And the Lapps cherish and reverence the memory of him who was the means of awakening many among them to a spiritual life.

A religious movement has manifested itself also

among the colonists from Finland who have settled in this region. Mr. Laing speaks of this in his Tour in Sweden. A passage from his journal while in this northern region, presents such an interesting picture of these poor Christians engaged in their simple religious exercises, that we cannot refrain from transcribing it here.

"Degenfors, July, 1838. I got up very early this morning, and went down to the rapids or *fors* of the river* to fish. I came unexpectedly upon a party of six or eight men, women, and young people, gathered in a snug hollow of the river bank, which only an angler would have thought of visiting at so early an hour. One man, with his hat off, was reading the Bible to the others, and just concluding and shutting the book. They seemed in a little confusion, until they saw that I was fishing and taking no notice of them. When my landlord came to join me with his fishing rod, and they found that I was lodging with him, and not at the *manse*—and they asked the question—they seemed pleased. There is, I had heard, a religious enthusiasm spreading itself in the north of Sweden, especially among the colonists or new settlers in Lapland, which the clergy attempt to put down and extinguish. These religionists are called Läsaren—the readers—from their reading the Scriptures, and must keep themselves quiet, because,

* The Wandel, one of the main branches of the Umea.

although they cannot be openly persecuted, and there is an enlightened and liberal public in Sweden, who would be roused, if any one was openly oppressed, on account of his religious opinions; yet, where the clergyman is all-powerful in his parish, and has the public functionaries to support him, there are many ways of making the poor man, who presumes to have either too much or too little religious zeal to suit the pastor, feel in his worldly concerns the ill consequences of wandering from the beaten church road."*

The events of subsequent years, as the reader of this little volume has perceived, have furnished a painful contradiction to Mr. Laing's opinion, that in Sweden a man cannot be openly persecuted and oppressed on account of his religious opinions. It is true, however, that there are enlightened and liberal men in Sweden, who deplore the persecuting spirit of the hierarchy, and enter a continual protest against it. Let us hope that their voice may at length be heard.

In 1859, Rev. Nas Per Person visited Lapland. He was there during the mouths of October and November, in a region within one degree of the Arctic Circle. He was received with joy. In every place large and interested congregations gathered around him, and the blessing of God accompanied his labors. We will give some extracts

* Laing's Sweden, p. 178.

from his journal; they give a vivid picture of the eagerness with which the people listen to the word of God.

"On the 26th of September, I left Sundsvall, by steamboat, and after a voyage of three hundred miles, arrived safely on the 29th, at the town of Pitea. This town is prettily situated upon the coast, and has about fifteen hundred and forty-five inhabitants. A small trade is carried on chiefly in timber.

"I was received with manifest tokens of joy by all the friends of Christ. In this town there is a great hungering to hear the word of God. 30th—I visited the sick at the hospital, and conversed with several believers, and with some who were anxiously seeking salvation. In the evening I preached; upwards of two hundred persons were present; nearly all were moved to tears; the Spirit of the Lord seemed to hover over the room. Believers greatly rejoiced, and continued long together in singing and prayer. None seemed willing to leave. October 1st—I visited several families, and then went to Old Pitea, distributing tracts on the way. Two women, whom I conversed with, wept bitterly over the sense of their sins. The dean of the town permitted me to preach in the public school-house. About five hundred were present; all were powerfully affected by the word."

The following day, Sunday, he preached in New Pitea, both morning and afternoon. In the afternoon nearly six hundred were present, and many were obliged to return home because they could not get in. Deep interest was manifested, and several were enabled to believe in Christ. The next morning he visited five families, in each family a number of friends had assembled, some of whom were weeping, desiring to find Christ, while others were greatly rejoicing in their Saviour. In the afternoon he preached to about four hundred persons. Christians in Pitea beheld with joy the interest that was awakened, and rejoiced over sinners turning to the Saviour.

The remainder of the week, Nas Per Person spent in visiting places in the neigborhood of Pitea. In every place the preaching of the word was listened to with eager interest. "At Innesmark," he writes, "many of the young people wept bitterly. I conversed with the young children, and requested a friend to hold Sunday-school with them." "At Blosmark, many young people were pricked in their hearts by the word, and many of the aged were melted to tears."

On Friday, 7th, he returned to Pitea, and preached in the evening to a very large congregation, among whom were the captain of the police, and many of the most respectable citizens of the town. At an early hour the following morning, before he was up, many came to the house desirous to converse with him on their eternal interests. Everywhere that he went, during that day, he found some weeping over their sins, and seeking the Saviour.

"Sunday, 9th, I preached in New Pitea, at 9, A. M., about four hundred were present. After worship I conversed with inquirers. We organized a Sunday-school of fifty children. Several of the children were awakened. In the afternoon, at five o'clock, I preached to a large congregation. The principal people in the place were present. I was told of a sailor who would not work to-day, but asked permission of the captain to go and hear preaching; the consequence was, that the captain and all the crew came to the meeting."

This week, like the preceding, he spent in visiting villages, from three to nine miles from Pitea, preaching and visiting from house to house. The following Sunday he returned to Pitea. The Sunday-school, organized the preceding week, now increased to one hundred and fifty children. Both parents and children wept when he spoke of Jesus. At five in the afternoon he preached, and again numbers were obliged to go home for want of room. The house could not contain more than six hundred, and in so high a latitude at that season, preaching in the open air was impossible.

He now left Pitea and went northward, preaching every where in the villages. "At Persnas," he says, "my hearers seemed cold and hardened. At the close of the sermon I went round and conversed with them, when many became deeply moved, and some of the young people wept bitterly, and said, 'we are the chief of sinners.'" He remained two days in this place, and before he left many expressed an anxious concern for their souls. On his return there, November 24th, he writes: "Preached in the afternoon at Persnas. I found that many had found peace in believing, since my last visit a month ago."

At one place, where many appeared much affected by the preaching of the word, an aged Christian exclaimed: "Now the prejudices against the Baptists will vanish." Strong prejudices against them exist among the Lutheran separatists. In two or three places, they persuaded the people not to open any rooms in which Nas Per Person might preach. But the people, in one place, when a room was thus refused to him, followed him to another village, At Afvan a room was refused to him, by five different families. At length a family opened their doors; about forty attended. He preached the next morning; a larger number came. In the evening upwards of one hundred were present. The next morning he preached in another house, in the same village, to two hundred people. After service, a man stood up and thanked him, in the name of the assembly, for what he had said, adding, "we have never heard such gospel truths in this northern region before." Many were now willing and anxious that he should preach in their houses; but he could not remain longer, as he had still many places to visit.

At Svansbyn the hearts of men were prepared to welcome the truths and consolations of the gospel by a solemn warning received a month before—twelve persons had been drowned in the Lulea River. Here Nas Per Person remained two days, preaching, and holding prayer meetings. Great religious interest prevailed, and much sorrow was manifested when he left the place.

In the parish of Ranea he was invited to stay at the house of the Rector of the parish. He preached three times in this place: nearly all the persons of the higher class attended, and among them two priests, and a district-sergeant. He also held a prayer-meeting in the house of the Rector. At Bole, also, he was invited to preach in the house of the Rector, and here he conversed with several inquirers.

At Borjeslandet, on a second visit, he writes:

"A Mrs. L. and her daughter, and the wife of a farmer, applied for baptism. I told them not to take the step hastily, but to count the cost. They were so desirous, and appeared so well grounded in the truth, that I could not put them off. After I had baptized them we celebrated the Lord's Supper together, rejoicing greatly in Christ our Saviour. 11th. I preached twice. I spoke publicly on church polity, and the sentiments held by the Baptists. There was no opposition. Two were enabled to rejoice in believing. 12th. Early in the morning some came to me whose hearts were overflowing with heavenly joy. Two days before a husband had beaten his wife because she wished to be baptized. To-day he is rejoicing in his Saviour, and humbly asks his wife's forgiveness." He writes at Old Lulea: "Sunday, 13th. As there were six baptized believers in this parish they were constituted into a church. We celebrated the Lord's Supper together. These are the only baptized believers found in the province of Norrbotten. May this little mustard-seed grow until it shall become a great tree! In the afternoon I preached: two hundred were present."

Thence he went to New Lulea, six miles distant. Here he was welcomed by the pastor of the State Church. We are struck with the wide difference between the conduct of the priests in Lapland, and in the other parts of Sweden. In Skänia the priest pursues him who dares to preach the word of God to perishing sinners, and a prison and chains ase his reward. In Lapland, in more than one instance, the priest welcomes the preacher of the gospel, invites him to his house, and accompanies him in his ministrations.

"New Lulea, Nov. 15th. I was kindly received by the pastor of the State Church, and others. I preached: about one hundred and fifty were present. The minds of the people had been very much prejudiced against me on account of evil reports circulated against the Baptists. They were, in fact, afraid of me; now, however, their prejudices have greatly diminished. 16th. I preached twice. A much larger number were present than on the preceding day. I conversed with several anxious souls. 17th. I made family visits, and preached twice. At the afternoon meeting the power of the Holy Ghost was felt to be in our midst. Between three and four hundred persons were present, and many were obliged to return home, as they could not obtain an entrance into the room. 18th. I preached in the morning: about sixty were present: several anxious inquirers came to converse with me. In the afternoon I preached at the prison; Pastor B. accompanied me. One of the prisoners wept over his sins. In the evening I again preached to about four hundred persons."

He then returned to Old Lulea, and preached in the afternoon to about three hundred persons. Some had found peace in believing during that week. The same evening, he went back to New Lulea, and preached there the following day.

"Sunday, 20th. I preached in the morning at eight o'clock; the room was filled. I heard Pastor B. preach in the State Church; he spoke with power. I organized a Sunday-school of fifty-five children. In the evening I preached again to a large congregation."

The following morning he left Lulea, and returned to Pitea, preaching in several villages by the way. At Rosvik, several refused at first to open their houses for a meeting, but, as he was leaving the village, they ran after the wagon, and begged him to remain. A number assembled to hear the word. And the following morning, when he again preached, many shed tears, mourning over their sins. Leaving, we may hope, some good seed in their hearts, the unwearied colporteur proceeded on his way.

He arrived at Pitea on the evening of the 25th. Here he heard glad tidings about the Sunday-school which had been organized about six weeks before.

"It has not only been continued, but has increased to two hundred children. Upwards of twenty of these children have found peace in believing, and others are under deep concern for their souls' salvation. Added to this, many of their parents have been converted during the last six weeks. Truly there is great joy in this city."

The following day he visited from house to house, and held three prayer-meetings. He also conversed with several who were earnestly considering the subject of baptism.

"Sunday, 27th. I preached in the morning: about three hundred were present. We held Sunday-school in the afternoon: one hundred and seventy children were present. The faces of many of these children were beaming with peace and joy;

others were weeping over their sins. In the evening, about five hundred persons assembled. I preached to them. Everywhere rejoicing faces were seen, indicative of that peace which the world can neither give nor take away, even the peace of Jesus."

CHAPTER XIV.

PERSECUTIONS.

In the days of the Apostles the seasons of persecution were the seasons of peculiar blessing. When, after the martyrdom of Stephen, "there was a great persecution against the Church . . . . they that were scattered abroad went everywhere preaching the word." When James was killed with the sword, and Peter was cast into prison, "the word of God grew and multiplied." And thus has it ever been; the sufferings of believers have been blessed to the conversion of sinners and the growth of the Church.

When England emerged from the darkness of Popery into the light of the Reformation, the fires of persecution were enkindled, and the blazing fagots of Smithfield and Oxford cast a lurid glare over that painful and difficult transit. When Scotland sought a purer mode of worship, her best and noblest sons were hunted into caves and glens, while some sealed their faith with their blood, and others languished out their lives in the dungeons of the Bass Rock.

We need not multiply the sad examples with

which the records of history are stained. But let us note this for our encouragement, and for the encouragement of our struggling, suffering brethren in Sweden. Wherever persecutions have abounded, the grace of God has yet more abounded. The faith of the persecuted has been strengthened, and the interests of Christ's kingdom have been advanced. This has been seen in days of old, and it is seen in our day in Sweden.

When Mr. Hejdenberg was arrested in the northern part of Sweden, and conveyed a prisoner, in company with thieves, nearly four hundred miles, to answer for the crime of having preached the gospel, his enemies meant to crush him, and to silence his voice. Yet how widely different was the result! From his prison cell, in Stockholm, came that touching appeal which awakened so deep an interest in the hearts of Christians in America, and won many zealous friends to the Baptist cause in Sweden.

Mr. Hejdenberg has been bitterly persecuted, and his labors in the cause of Christ have been greatly blessed. During the autumn of 1855, and the ensuing winter, he was summoned to appear before different courts, in distant parts of the country, fined no less than five times, imprisoned once for twenty-nine days; yet he labored unceasingly in preaching, though preaching and administering the ordinances constituted the sum of his offenses. Like the Apostles, though imprisoned for preaching he preached while in prison. During his journeys from court to court during that period—from August to April—he traveled two thousand four hundred and eighteen miles, held one hundred and forty-four religious meetings, and baptized one hundred and sixteen converts.

An interesting incident, which occurred during one of his imprisonments, will show how good may be effected, even under the most unfavorable circumstances. He was being carried as a prisoner to stand his trial.

On reaching Nyköping he was placed in a private room of the town jail. Whilst praying aloud, he heard a low, female voice in the next room. When he had finished his prayer the woman addressed him, telling him that she was very miserable, and that his prayer had made a deep impression on her. This gave rise to a conversation through the wall, which continued the greater part of the night. Mr. Hejdenberg strove to point this distressed and anxious sinner to the Lamb of God, and he had reason to hope that his efforts were blessed of God to her conversion. The next morning they took leave of each other without having met. They may probably never see each other's faces on earth, yet, throughout all eternity, that woman may have cause to bless God for that night in the prison.

Notwithstanding persecutions, fines, and imprisonments, Mr. Hejdenberg's course has been steadily onward. He is now pastor of the Baptist church in Sundsvall. This church, we find by reference to the statistics of the churches in Sweden for 1858, numbers one hundred and sixty-seven members: forty-five were added by baptism during that year.

In 1856, a strong effort was made to secure liberty of conscience. King Oscar, on the assembling of the Diet, Oct. 17th, 1856, used the following words, which caused a thrill of joy to many Christian hearts, and raised, in the minds of the much-persecuted Baptists, hopes which were but too soon crushed. These are his words:

"Toleration, founded on individual, immovable conviction, and respect for the religious faith of others, belongs to the essence of the Protestant Church, and ought to obtain among a people whose heroic king, Gustavus Adolphus, by brilliant victories and the sacrifice of his life, laid the foundation of freedom of thought in central Europe. Those laws, therefore, which hinder religious liberty and freedom of worship, ought to be abolished, and general law be brought into closer harmony with the sixteenth section of the Constitution."*

The following incidents, narrated in a letter bear-

* The sixteenth section of the Constitution of 1809, to which the King refers, is as follows: "The King shall not coerce any man's conscience, nor suffer it to be coerced; but shall protect every one in the free exercise of his religion, so long as he does not disturb the peace, or occasion public scandal." The Constitution grants religious liberty, but this law of liberty has never been carried out.

ing date Oct. 18th, 1856, show how little regard was paid to this section of the Constitution of 1809:

"Klocklar Lars Person has just returned from the prison of Fahlun, after having been imprisoned on bread and water, because he had allowed Hejdenberg to read the Bible in his cottage." Certainly it is difficult to perceive wherein this "disturbed the peace, or occasioned public scandal."

"Nas Per Person has also again lately been fined one hundred rix-dollars, for holding conventicles; and his mother twenty-five rix-dollars, for taking the Lord's Supper out of the State Church."

At Motala, on Lake Wettern, Corlander was seized and thrown into a dungeon, where he was confined for six days. All these persecutions and imprisonments only caused these devoted Christians to labor yet more earnestly and zealously to preach the word, "in season and out of season," and brought them to cling yet more closely to the consolations of the gospel. One of them, on leaving his prison cell, thus expresses his feelings on entering it:

"The precious words of promise were applied with power to my heart: 'Behold I am with you.' 'None shall pluck you from my hand.' I thought of poor Bunyan, who had, for twelve years, been confined in a prison, and also of Bro. Hejdenberg, who has been twice confined in this dismal place."

The noble and truly Protestant language of King

Oscar seemed to stir up the spirit of persecution and intolerance to still greater outrages.

In Skänia (the most southern province of Sweden), where, during the spring of 1857, nearly three hundred believers had been baptized, every effort was made to silence the preaching of the gospel. The authorities seized and imprisoned Baptist preachers, wherever found without the limits of their own parish. During this spring, six colporteurs were at various times confined in the Cell-prison at Christianstad, some of whom were treated very harshly.

One of these, a blind colporteur, named Nils Hokanson, was confined for eight days, for circulating religious books and tracts. After his release, an iron chain was attached to one of his ankles. It was intended that this chain should be fastened around both ankles, but he was allowed the privilege of walking and carrying one end of it in his hand. After this he was taken on a prison car to another station, where new irons were placed on him. In this condition he was sent to his home, where the authorities compelled him to pay a considerable sum, to compensate them for the trouble of bringing him home. As he had no money wherewith to satisfy their claim, they seized that which he had received from book sales, and also a watch which he wore, which had been loaned to him.

Sven Svenson, of whose faithful and successful

labors in Skänia an account is given in Chapter X., was subjected to cruel imprisonments. On a second imprisonment, after having being stripped of all his clothing, they washed his body in cold water, cut his hair close to his head—a course of treatment to which criminals are subjected—and severely buffeted him with their fists. Then, having clothed him in a prisoner's dress, they threw him into a cold, damp cell. Severe chills seized him, when the door of the dark cell was suddenly closed upon him; rebellious thoughts began to rise, but, says he, "I threw myself on my knees imploring Jesus, my Saviour, to be with me, and let me see light in His light. Then the prison became no longer a prison to me, but all was peace, light, and joy."

Another Colporteur, Helge Okeson, was treated in a similar manner.

The hopes of greater religious toleration, which had been raised by the king's speech, and by the efforts which had been put forth by the friends of liberty of conscience, were soon entirely crushed.

After the lapse of two years, in October, 1858, an act was passed, which pressed still more heavily on all who sought to worship God according to the dictates of their conscience. The old law of banishment for religious dissent was retained. The Conventical Act of 1726 was repealed, and the new act invested "the Church Council" in every parish, with power to prohibit any religious meetings, which, in their judgment, were likely to alienate the minds of the people from the State Church. Under the old act, the sanction of the Royal Chancellor of Justice was necessary, before proceedings could be instituted. Under the new act, prohibitions, fines, and imprisonments, were all at the discretion of the Church Council, which consists of the priest, and a few members selected by the priest himself.

The result may easily be anticipated. The spirit of persecution received a new impulse. Many, in various parts of the country, suffered fines and imprisonment. Several pastors, for administering baptism, or the Lord's Supper, were fined one hundred and fifty rix-dollars, or imprisoned for twenty-eight days, on bread and water. The extreme difficulty which frequently attends the administration of the Lord's Supper, may be seen from the following narrative.

Colporteur Lundquist went to the parish of Godegord to preach. The place which was selected for the meeting was a small cottage buried in the woods. The disciples came together. From the seclusion of the spot they hoped to be able, unmolested, to enjoy the privileges of prayer and praise, of listening to the preaching of the gospel, and sitting around the table of the Lord. But the persecutors had tracked their steps. The little cottage in the woods was surrounded and forcibly entered. The minister of Christ was seized, and dragged with brutal violence from the house. The little congregation was dispersed, and the Christian woman, who had opened her house for the worship of God, was assailed not only with abuse but even with blows.

Mr. Lundquist was then driven into the woods for a distance of three or four miles; here he was detained prisoner until morning, when he was taken into the parish of Serback and set at liberty. It was not until evening that he succeeded in getting any food, and then he attempted to preach the word. After some days he reached home without books, and almost without clothes; for he had but one coat with him, and that they tore in pieces when they dragged him out of the cottage.

Undismayed by all he had undergone, Mr. Lundquist again attempted to administer the Lord's Supper. After losing his way in a deep swamp he came to a little hut, where he received permission to remain over night. But when the people of the house discovered that he was a Baptist, they became so much alarmed that they obliged him to leave the house, and seek a shelter elsewhere. The following day he succeeded in reaching his destination. The news of his arrival spread; the little church came together. But before the celebration of the Lord's Supper, Mr. Lundquist was again dragged out of the house, and the services were again forcibly closed.

These imprisonments, fines, blows, and cruel mockings, are not the only forms of persecution to which the Baptists in Sweden are subjected. With grief we behold in our day, and in a church bearing the name of the great Reformer, the same spirit manifested which has ever animated Papal Rome,—the spirit of tyrannical rule over the consciences of men. This led her, in former ages, by rack and screw, by dungeons and by flames, to seek to retain men under her yoke; and this leads the clergy of Sweden, in our day, to use all their power to urge on their people ingeniously to devise every possible form of oppression and cruelty, whereby to coerce the conscience.

The following passage from a letter from Rev. A. S. Rechnitzer, of whose labors in the Island of Gottland, an account has been given in Chapter XI., affords evidence of this sad truth.

"The warfare in which the Baptists are engaged, is not alone with the world; but, even the pious members of the State Church are working against us unitedly. The priests keep themselves busy in persecuting the Baptists. Their hatred continues unabated. The children of Baptists are taken by force and sprinkled, while police officers stand godfathers for them. The priests have tried to have the names of the Baptists stricken out from the annual register, by that means depriving them of the rights of citizenship, but they have failed in their efforts. Being deposed from office, denied the loan of money from banks, or institutes; or, if a loan has been obtained on a former occasion, forced to immediate repayment; such are some of the every-day transactions against the Baptists. Thus the external circumstances of the Baptists are exceedingly trying. Some of our brethren have been so pressed, that they have been obliged to sell the little property they owned for one-third of its value, so as to make immediate payment to those who had demands against them."

It is pleasing to see that other modes, besides fines and imprisonment, are to be tried for the reclamation of the Baptists. It is a sign of better things, when arguments from the sacred Scriptures are employed to enlighten heretics. The following extract from "Evangelical Christendom," of Dec., 1859, will be read with interest in this connection:

"A new method of dealing with the Swedish Baptists has been ordered by the King in Council. In August last the Consistory of Westeras memorialized the Government, requesting instruction how to proceed with the large number of Baptists found in the parish of Hedemora; to which the Government have replied, that if the labors of the ordinary clergy to reclaim these persons by serious, constant, and loving instruction, are insufficient, the Consistory must immediately send to that parish a clergyman eminently gifted for this work, who will, for the time, receive his support from the State, and that a report of the result shall be sent to Stockholm after six months have elapsed. It is already known that the Consistories of Upsala and Lund have represented to the Government the importance of obtaining from the next Diet a grant of public money for the support of such 'traveling preachers,' and the directions forwarded to Westeras indicate the mind of the Government on the matter.

"The Rev. Archdeacon Eklundh, of Hudiksvall, has been sent by the Consistory of Upsala to Hassela, in Helsingland, where a meeting of Baptists was held last midsummer, attended by about six hundred adherents from ten parishes. Several were baptized during the meeting, and about three hundred united in 'breaking of bread.' Mr. E. did not reach the place till the end of August, and spent two days in the parish church discussing with the Baptists, in the presence of large congregations, the points on which they differ from the Lutheran Church. The Baptists, with their pastors, attended in considerable numbers; and Mr. E. testifies that, with the exception of the sacrament of Baptism, the work of the Spirit in the conversion of the sinner, the constitution of a Christian church, and the call to the ministry, their views harmonized with the standards of the Swedish Church, whilst their moral conduct was irreproachable. The visitation, which closed with an earnest exhortation to the Baptists to reconsider their position, did not lead, so far as is yet known, to the restoration of any of the separatists to communion with the National Church."

We have seen some of the persecutions which

the Baptists in Sweden have been compelled to suffer. Yet in a great fight of afflictions they have remained unshaken, and have steadily gained ground, as the preceding narrative abundantly shows. Their faith and patience may be tried for years to come, as they have been, and now are, but they may calmly trust in God, who has hitherto upheld them. His power and His goodness can, at no distant day, open to them a fairer field, and His word in that land may more rapidly run and be glorified. There are abundant signs of promise. The vision may, nevertheless, tarry; but we may confidently hope that for the Baptists of Sweden there is a future—a future fraught with peace and prosperity to themselves, and with blessings, through their instrumentality, to the Scandinavian races.

APPENDIX.

BAPTIST CHURCHES IN SWEDEN.

No. on Map.	CHURCHES.	PROVINCES.	Organized.	No. of Members, March, 1860.
1.	Lulea	Norrbotten's Lan.	1860	13
2.	Grunsunda	Hernosand's Lan.	1857	10
3.	Ramsele	(or Wester-	1859	5
4.	Helgum	Norrland's.)	1857	32
5.	Ljustorp	" "	1856	64§
6.	Stafre, parish of Ljustorp	" "	1860	24
7.	Hassjo	" "	1857	22§
8.	Indal	" "	1860	13
9.	Timra	" "	1856	34§
10.	Skon	" "	1858	28
11.	Alnon	" "	1860	10
12.	Sundsvall	" "	1855	167
13.	Skallbole, parish of Tuna	" "	1856	40
14.	Tunbyn, parish of Tuna	" "	1858	16
15.	Njurunda	" "	1858	17§
16.	Attmar	" "	1857	72
17.	Hamre, parish of Attmar	" "	1860	22
18.	Carlang, parish of Attmar	" "	1860	31
19.	Stode	" "	1856	103
20.	Gransjo, parish of Stode	" "	1856	48
21.	Romback, parish of Torp	" "	1859	21§
22.	Knutnaset, parish of Torp	" "	1858	17§
23.	Hjeltanstorp, parish of Torp	" "	1857	31
24.	Ragunda	Jemtland's Lan.	1856	37
25.	As	" "	1857	25§
26.	Klappe, parish of Marby	" "	1857	20§
27.	Nas	" "	1858	18§
28.	Hackas	" "	1858	9§
29.	Hassela	Gefleborg's Lan.	1856	81
30.	Lindsjon, parish of Hassela	" "	1856	69
31.	Stensjon, parish of Hassela	" "	1858	30
*32.	Furuberg, parish of Bjuraker	" "	1859	24

* *Furuberg*, west from Stensjon, between Hassela elf and Svaga elf.

33. Gnarp	Gefleborg's	Lan....	1857	57§
34. Bergsjo	"	"	1856	61§
35. Ilsbo	"	"	1857	25
36. Hudiksvall	"	"	1858	26
37. Forssa	"	"	1856	9§
38. Rengsjo	"	"	1857	17§
39. Alfta	"	"	1858	32§
40. Gefle	"	"	1858	9
41. Elfdalen	Fahlu,	Lan....	1854	200§
42. Orsa	"	"	1854	254
43. Wamhus	"	"	1855	180§
44. Bonas, parish of Mora	"	"	1857	68
45. Ona, parish of Mora	"	"	1854	56§
46. Hedemora	"	"	1859	52
47. Ullerud	Carlstad's,	Lan....	1858	25
48. Nyed	"	"	1859	27
49. Fogelvik	"	"	1858	38
50. Hult, parish of Amneharad	Mariestad's	Lan....	1859	9
51. Orebro	Orebro,	Lan....	1854	115
52. Stora Mellosa	"	"	1859	65
53. Asker	"	"	1858	21§
54. Skyllersta	"	"	1859	20§
55. Kumla	"	"	1859	20
56. Wiby	"	"	1856	38§
57. Lerback	"	"	1860	7
58. Askersund	"	"	1859	10
59. Arboga	Westeras'	Lan....	1859	11
60. Ostuna	Stockholm's	Lan....	1859	10
61. Beateberg, parish of Roo	"	"	1859	26
62. Sigtuna	"	"	1857	40§
63. Stockholm	"	"	1855	150
64. Strengnas	Nykoping's	Lan....	1858	26
65. Broby, parish of Tumbo	"	"	1859	12
66. Westra Wingaker	"	"	1859	18
67. Regna	Linkoping's	Lan....	1859	8
68. Hellestad	"	"	1854	25§
69. Godegard	"	"	1858	6§
70. Motala	"	"	1856	14§
71. Norrkoping	"	"	1856	27
72. Hallingeberg	Calmar,	Lan....	1859	25
73. Westervik	"	"	1859	16
74. Wimmerby	"	"	1858	14
75. Wisby	Gottland's	Lan....	1858	32
76. Trakumla	"	"	1859	28
77. Hafdhem	"	"	1858	132
78. Grotlingbo	"	"	1859	38
79. Nas	"	"	1859	32
80. Hamra	"	"	1858	111
81. Torpa	Halmstad's	Lan....	1849	27
82. Issjoa, parish of Hamneda	Wexio,	Lan....	1857	18
83. Bohult, parish of Kinneryd	(or Kronoberg's.)		1859	33
84. Carlshamn	Carlskrona	Lan....	1856	9§
85. Solvesborg	"	"	1859	16§
86. Werum	Christianstad's	Lan.	1857	10§
87. Mala, parish of Wankifva	"	"	1857	131
88. Horja	"	"	1859	10§
89. Broby	"	"	1857	50
90. Tagarod, parish of Hjersas	"	"	1857	64

*91. Perstorp, parish of Oppmanna....	Christianstad's Lan.	1859	28
†92. Odersberga, parish of Fjelkestad.	" "	1860	16
93. Grodby, parish of Ifvetofta.........	" "	1857	30§
94. Ullstorp, parish of Onnesta.........	" "	1857	135
95. Christianstad	" "	1857	41
96. Wenesta, parish of Trane..	" "	1857	24
97. Gringelsta, parish of Kopinge.....	" "	1858	16
‡98. Illenstorp, parish of W. Wram...	" "	1859	14
99. Yngsjo, parish of Ahus.............	" "	1857	95
100. Brosarp...................................	" "	1857	47
101. Killerod, parish of Ostraby.........	Malmohus Lan....	1857	46
102. Foglo..	Aland, (Russia).......	1857	8§
Baptized, but not connected with any church..			80
Probable increase in churches from which no statistics have been received this year, and which are marked thus (§)			200
	Sum Total	......	4548

* *Perstorp*, north from Oppmanna, near to Vanga.
† *Odesberga*, at Helga, just between Hjersas and Osterlof.
‡ *Illenstorp*, southwest from W. Wram, east from Maltesholm.

SUMMARY.

Jan. 1856,	Churches	..................12.	Members	476
" 1857,	"	..................21.	"	961
" 1858,	"	..................45.	"	 2105
" 1859,	"	..................69.	"	 3487
" 1860,	"	................102.	"	 4548

LIST OF COLPORTEURS IN SWEDEN,

SUPPORTED BY THE AMERICAN BAPTIST PUBLICATION SOCIETY.

Rev. A. Wiberg, Stockholm, Superintendent.
" Gustaf Palmquist.
" Nas Per Person.
" Sas Per Person.
" Jonas Petter Lundquist.
" Sven Svenson.
" Frederick Forst.
" Axel Schamil Rechnitzer.
" Frederick Rymcker.
" Andrew John Hanner.
" Carl Magnus Carlander.
" Per Ulrik Wahlberg.
" Andreas Magnus Claeson.
" F. O. Nilsson.
" Charles Mollersvard, supported by the Mariners' Baptist Church, New York City.

www.ingramcontent.com/pod-product-compliance
Lightning Source LLC
LaVergne TN
LVHW021200120826
845150LV00011B/1457

* 9 7 8 1 4 2 5 5 1 6 8 8 8 *